SEX IN NATURE

SEX IN NATURE

CHRIS CATTON & JAMES GRAY

Facts On File Publications
New York, New York ● Oxford, England

if so this is
manuscript
would like
to thank Michael Chamberlain and Rachel Stewart for
reading the first draft of the whole book, pointing out
confusing passages and making many helpful
suggestions, and Michael Festenstein whose intelligent
criticism has been invaluable. Thanks are also due to Sue
Baker, for more beautiful drawings, to Mary Anne
Sanders for constant help and encouragement, to the staff
of the Radcliffe Science Library, the Science Reference
Library and the Natural History Museum. Above all, our
thanks to the friends and families who have kept us going.

This book was designed and produced by
The Oregon Press Limited, Faraday House,
8 Charing Cross Road, London WC2H 0HG

Copyright © Green Films Limited 1985

First published in the United States of America by
Facts on File Publications, 460 Park Avenue South,
New York, N.Y. 10016

ISBN 0-8160-1294-6

Design: Gail Engert

Filmset by SX Composing Limited, Rayleigh, England
Origination by Waterdens Reproductions Limited, London
Printed and bound by Clark Constable Limited, Edinburgh

HALF-TITLE *Common blue butterflies courting (Polyommatus icarus)*
FRONTISPIECE *Courtship dance of the European crane (Grus grus)*

Contents

Acknowledgments

The story of sex in nature could never have been told were it not for the work of the many, many zoologists, botanists and other specialists from all over the world from whose work we have drawn so heavily, and without whose philosophizing we could not have interpreted the very few observations we ourselves have been lucky enough to make. One or other of these scientists is indirectly responsible for almost every line in this book, but to acknowledge their contributions fully would take an appendix half as long again. So we hope that they will forgive us for referring those readers who are particularly interested in who did what, to a few rather more technical (but still very readable) books, where many of the papers we have consulted are listed in full:

An Introduction to Behavioural Ecology, John R. Krebs and Nick B. Davies (Blackwell, 1981)
Sex, Evolution and Behaviour, Martin Daly and Margo Wilson (W. Grant P., 1983)
The Sex Life of Flowers, Bastiaan Meeuse and Sean Morris (Faber, 1984)
Sociobiology and Behaviour, David P. Barash (Hodder, 1982)
Sociobiology: The New Synthesis, Edward O. Wilson (Harvard U.P., 1980)

We would also like to acknowledge a special debt to Dr Tim Halliday, author of *Sexual Strategy* (Oxford U.P., 1980) which provided the original inspiration for the film on insect sexual behaviour in which this book had its beginnings.

We must beg forgiveness for our often unscientific language. We have deliberately chosen to avoid jargon so that as many people as possible can share in the discoveries that make up the story. In doing so we have often spoken of plants and animals as if they were conscious beings, capable of making decisions and planning strategies. We hope it is adequately clear in the text that this is only a matter of style, and in our defence can do no better than quote James Lloyd, one of the active scientists whose work on fireflies is largely responsible for the jam on the bread of 'Sight':

> What harm is done if I speak of a firefly thinking, or blowing his little mind? ... Catching an author in a conceptual error of substance is more productive and more enjoyable, and has greater reward, than complaining that he speaks of insects in terms appropriate to little people.

Introduction

Black rhinoceroses mating. Rhinoceroses have long been a symbol of sexual potency, and for years these magnificent animals have been hunted for their horn. The numbers of some species, like the Indian one-horned rhinoceros, have fallen rapidly, causing serious concern for their future. It is slightly ironic that only by studying their sexual behaviour have conservationists been able to prevent their extinction.

Sex

Mating for the rhinoceros is a serious and lengthy business. The male begins his courtship of the female by gently nudging her with the side of his head and jabbing her beneath the belly with his horn. When she is suitably aroused, he mounts and the pair begins an energetic frolic during which the male can ejaculate ten times or more before climbing down some half an hour later. This then is sex in the natural world, raw and unashamed. It is we humans who have found magic, myth and metaphor in the mating rhinos.

The magic of the rhino lies in its horn, which can be ground to a powder that is a potent aphrodisiac, at least according to the first explorers who returned from Asia with many a tale to tell. The horn has long been credited with different magical properties in Africa, central Asia and the Far East, where it was fashioned into elaborately carved cups used by paranoid rulers to neutralize poison in their drinks. The practice even spread to Europe, where rhino-horn cups were used by popes and monarchs.

There are two myths about the value of the rhinoceros' horn as a sexual stimulant. Not surprisingly, the tea brewed and bragged about by Victorian hunters has no effect on the human libido; after all, the horn is made of exactly the same tissue as fingernails, hardly the stuff to generate unrestrained passion. The idea that the horn has ever been widely used as a sexual stimulant is also a myth. Horn now fetches $17,000 a kilo (2.2 lb) in Taiwan, but far from setting the local menfolk panting, it is valued for its imagined properties as a fever-reducing drug. The supposed aphrodisiac powers are a relatively recent invention. Westerners, puzzled by its presence on the shelves of herbalists, probably jumped to the wrong conclusions on account of its phallic shape.

The horn is used as a metaphor only in the Yemen, where it is made into dagger handles, status symbols for young men who have come of age, but it is this comparatively innocent use that now threatens the very survival of the rhinoceros. Financed by the oil wealth of the Persian Gulf, trade in rhinoceros horn is thriving, while back home in Africa and Asia, populations are dwindling. Man's imagination has linked the rhinoceros' horn with sex and maturity, a link with the power of generation that could ironically lead to the extinction of these magnificent animals. By seriously studying their breeding biology, conservationists have been able to save at least one of the endangered species. Numbers of the one-horned Indian rhinoceros have swelled in the past few years, thanks to careful protection and a thorough knowledge of their behaviour. But much more work remains to be done if the Javan rhino, of which less than sixty specimens remain, is to share the same secure future.

At the other extreme, prying into the sexual habits of animals has dramatically reduced the damaging effects of some pests. One of the most serious insect pests of livestock in the southern United States, the screw-worm, has been eradicated by releasing large numbers of

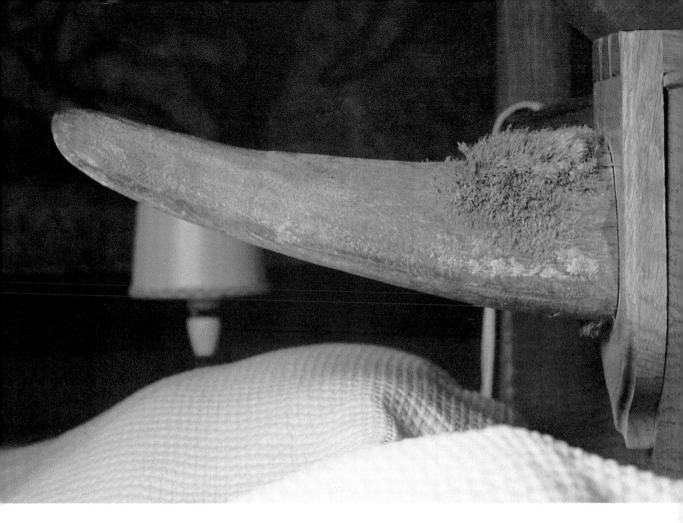

A large rhinoceros horn mounted on a headboard in the 'Kama Sutra' bedroom of Lord Weymouth's apartments at Longleat.

irradiated, sterile males into the population, while the production of synthetic sex attractants allows farmers to lure plant pests like the boll weevil and the cabbage looper moth to their death, so reducing the hazard and expense of spraying the crop.

The study of sex has produced dramatic results, but the ideas about how and why plants and animals reproduce as they do are enthralling even when they have no practical applications for humans at all. This book is intended to bring these ideas to a wider audience.

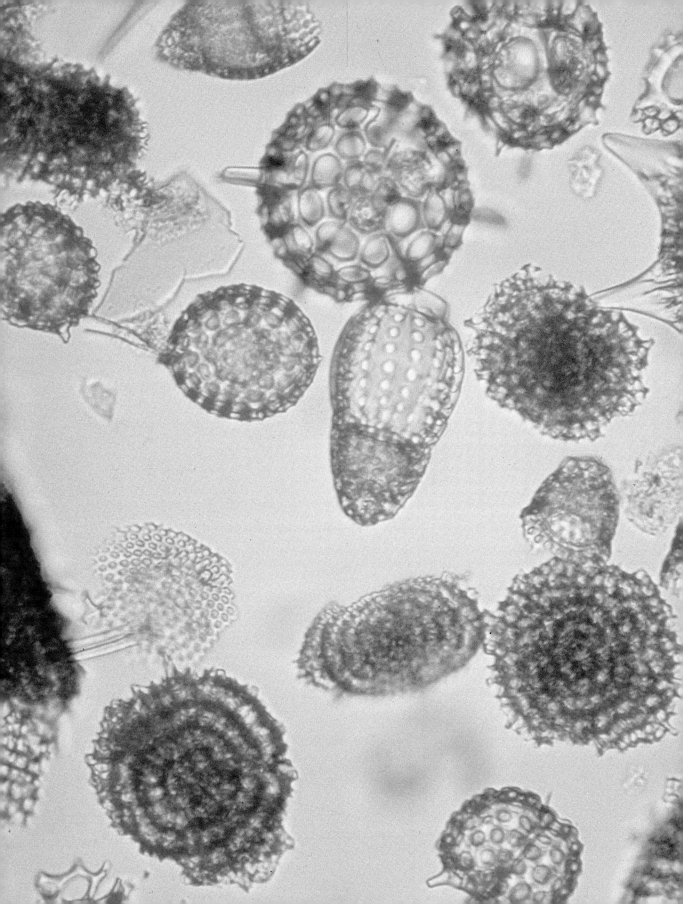

chapter one

The Beginnings of Sex

Some simple creatures may never have reproduced sexually. For instance, sexual reproduction is unknown in the radiolarians, the minute marine animals that built these intricate shells. While it is possible that these creatures once developed sexual reproduction only to discard it later, it is perhaps more likely that they represent a part of the animal kingdom that has never evolved sex at all. Though their skeletons are beautiful, the radiolarians have remained as minute and simple creatures for millions of years, and it is the animals and plants that reproduced sexually that have gone on to create the natural world with which we are most familiar.

Crude Beginnings

So much that is beautiful in the natural world is connected with sex that it is tempting to imagine that Mother Nature herself gained some unique pleasure from it. Without sex, flowers would have no smell, there would be no chorus of birdsong at dawn, no brightly coloured butterflies and our whole world would be a grey shadow of its present beauty and variety. So let us first spare a thought for the world where that grey life still goes on, for there are many animals and plants that have apparently never evolved sex.

Because they are mostly small and single celled, we call these life-forms 'primitive', although the word is misleading in many ways. Obviously they are adapted to their niche in the present natural world, not to life in some distant past, and they have undergone many changes since the paths of single- and multi-celled organisms diverged from their common ancestor so many millions of years ago. In fact, calling them 'primitive' tells us less about these creatures than about our traditionally self-important view of nature as a hierarchy with man at the top. But whatever the changes that time has wrought, these simple organisms show us one thing very clearly: life without sex is possible and often very successful.

Perhaps the best known of these sexless creatures is the amoeba, common not only in schools but in ponds too, where it crawls around on the bottom, eating practically anything it can get its body around. When it has finished eating, it divides into two, each daughter cell receiving identical copies of the genetic material, the information package that says 'how to be an amoeba'. (See panel overleaf.)

Because the daughters' genes are the same as the parent's, the daughters are twins and when they in turn divide, their progeny too is identical. The whole family is a clone, able to survive in precisely the same conditions as its parents, and all with precisely the same limitations. Only if there has been a mistake in the copying can a daughter cell be different, and such is the precision of DNA replication that mistakes are very rare. But they do occasionally happen, and when they do they are called mutations. Any mistake in copying a gene means that the protein for which that gene holds the code will be altered slightly. Usually this is a change for the worse, which will make the protein useless at its task. If a mutation occurs that changes the enzyme which breaks down glucose, the amoeba will no longer be able to feed on this sugar. All amoebae carrying this mutation will be worse off, because they can no longer exploit such a wide range of foods. But very, very occasionally, a mutation occurs which is actually helpful. For instance the enzyme which breaks down glucose might be changed so that it now acts on a wider range of sugars, and a new strain of amoeba is created that can now survive in situations where its ancestors could not. The amoeba has evolved.

Such a completely asexual lifestyle is not restricted to animals. The mats of blue-green algae that cover the bottoms of ponds are also formed simply by repeated cell division. Some algae divide repeatedly

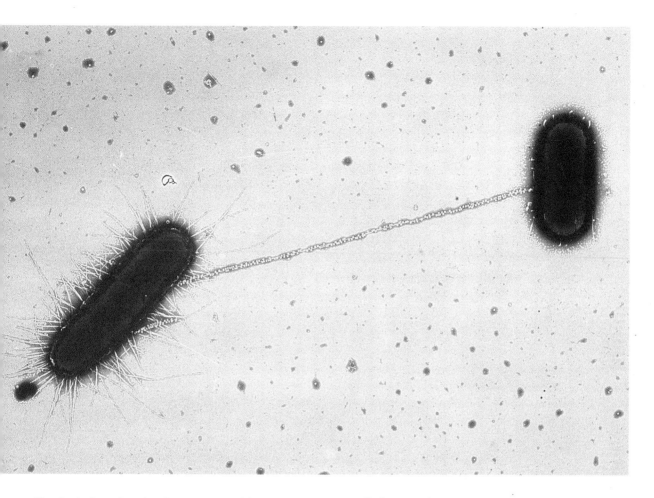

Two bacteria conjugating. Between them is the conjugation tube down which the genetic material passes from one cell to the other. See page 18.

without separating at all, forming long filaments. Chlorella, the green alga that sometimes forms a coating on tree-trunks, is also asexual, but in this case the daughter cells often remain within the same cell, so that a small colony is formed. Some other asexual algae remain glued together after dividing, forming clumps of cells. The radiolarians, marine Protozoa with bizarre and extravagant skeletons, divide by multiple fission, each fully grown cell dividing repeatedly to produce many small offspring. But in one essential sense the result is the same for all these plants and animals. Unless the DNA has mutated during the process of copying, all the daughters will be the same as their parents.

Only by mutating can amoebae or any other asexual organism produce anything totally new. Although mutations occur only rarely, and many are immediately lethal, it is through the incorporation of these accidental changes into the genetic material that many asexual life-forms have evolved. Yet even among single-celled plants and animals, there are only a few groups that reproduce exclusively without sex.

How to be an amoeba

The blueprint for making an amoeba is contained in its genes, each of which holds the code for making some part of the cell itself. The genes themselves are stretches of DNA (deoxyribonucleic acid), stuck together end to end to form enormously long strands which are tightly coiled into the structures known as chromosomes. Except in the bacteria and blue-green algae, these are packed into a separate bag inside the cell called the nucleus. As the amoeba grows, the genetic material (DNA) begins to reproduce itself. Each strand must be copied faithfully, for the DNA is the library to which the daughter amoebae will refer for instructions on how to manufacture new cell materials, and when the amoeba divides each daughter cell receives identical copies of the full library.

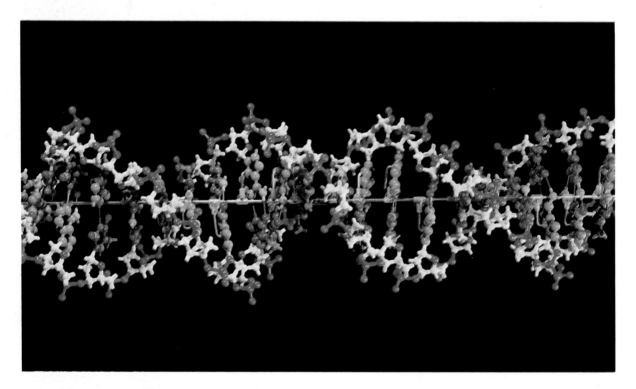

ABOVE *This model represents a short section of a DNA molecule, enough to carry the code for about a tenth of a small protein. On the same scale, a full chromosome might stretch a hundred and fifty kilometres (90 miles) or more. Yet in reality this much DNA is packed into cells invisible to the naked eye.*

OPPOSITE *A green alga dividing asexually to produce two identical cells. The DNA has already copied itself and a wall is now forming which will separate the daughters.*

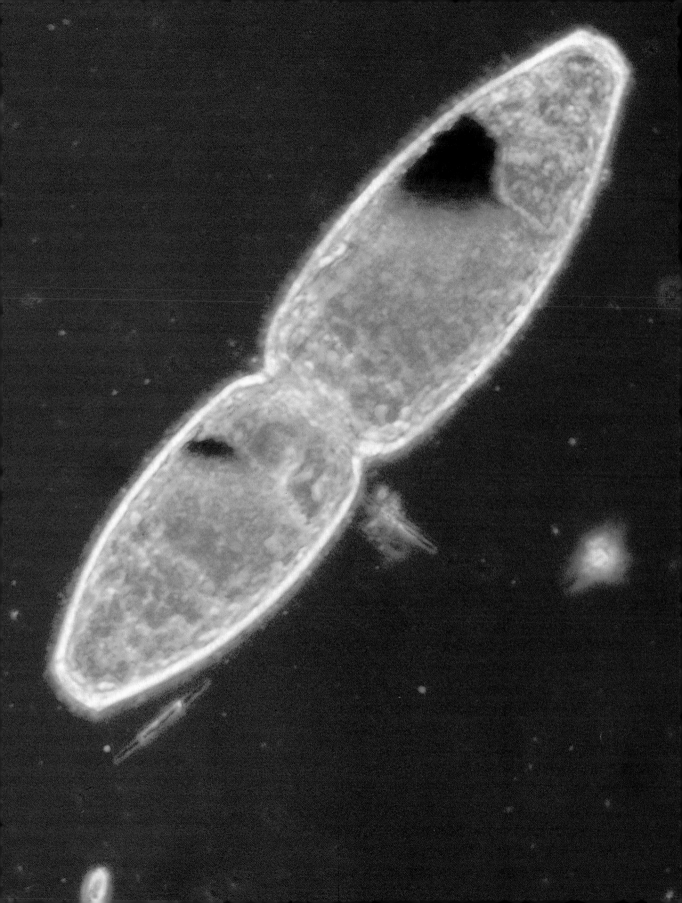

Conjugation among bacteria

Without sex, all the individuals of a population live in complete isolation from each other and are quite incapable of combining good evolutionary ideas. Individual amoebae may change through muta- tion, and if the mutations are beneficial these individuals may have more surviving offspring than their competitors. They might be so efficient that eventually the parent strain becomes extinct. But if two separate amoebae carry mutations, both of which are advantageous, there is no way that these can be combined in a single animal until at some future date the second mutation occurs in one of the daughters. The advantage that a sexual species has over an asexual species is that, through sex, favourable changes can be combined in a single organism.

Probably the simplest organisms to have developed a system for combining favourable mutations are the bacteria. Bacteria do not really reproduce sexually, that is to say sex between bacteria does not result in more bacteria being formed. But they can join together to pool information, combining genes from different individuals without increasing their numbers. This process – in effect having sex without reproducing – is called conjugation.

Those species of bacteria which can conjugate can be divided into two 'sexes', not exactly male and female, but donors and recipients, and during the process of conjugation, the donor connects with the recipient using a specially developed grappling-spike on its surface. (See illustration, page 15.)

The donor then copies its DNA, sending one copy down the conjugal bridge and retaining the other. As a result, the bacteria on the re- ceiving end can inherit all the traits of the donor. They also acquire the ability to donate DNA to other recipients: sex between bacteria changes their gender. The process is crude, since the pair is often separated before transfer is complete; but occasionally it does allow the combination of two favourable mutations in a single cell.

Bacterial conjugation has probably been going on for millions of years, but only in the last few decades have we humans begun to show serious interest. This simple, almost primeval version of sex has actually become a threat, because one consequence of conjugation in bacteria has been the appearance and rapid spread of strains which are resistant to a range of antibiotics. Resistance to a single antibiotic can easily arise in bacteria through mutation, but these bacteria can just as easily be killed off when hit with a different antibiotic. Multiple resistance is much more of a problem, since the more drugs disease- causing bacteria are resistant to, the fewer are the options for treat- ment. These strains with multiple resistance probably arose by the sexual combination of several separate mutations, and certainly they are now transmitted to recipient bacteria by conjugation.

Many bacterial infections that could until recently be cured with specific antibiotics are today resistant to treatment with the same drugs, and not surprisingly the spread of these resistant strains is being closely studied.

Simple Sex

The sexual process in bacteria is extremely crude. A bacterium which has received a batch of DNA by conjugating might have received a useful mutation. It also receives extra copies of material which it already had, and which must now be written out twice every time the bacterium divides. But early in evolutionary history, between 800 and 1000 million years ago, a new system appeared which involved not donation of genetic material by one organism to another, but an equal exchange of material between the two.

This system still exists in a simple form in the single-celled alga, *Chlamydomonas reinhardti*. These tiny plants reproduce for most of their lives in the same way as the amoeba, simply by splitting in two. But when life in the pond gets tough, they change. The wall around each cell dissolves, and they join together in pairs linked by a narrow fertilization tube. The whip-like flagellae, which normally propel the cell through the water, remain intact throughout the process. At first they beat in uncoordinated confusion, and the pair swim in circles, but slowly they begin to move in unison once more, and the pair can swim through the water until the cells fuse and become completely surrounded by a single, spiky wall. At this stage the genetic material of both the parent algae is contained within this wall. The new cell is

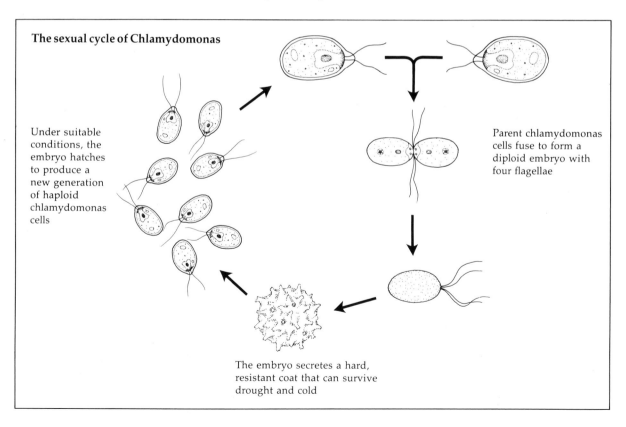

The sexual cycle of Chlamydomonas

Under suitable conditions, the embryo hatches to produce a new generation of haploid chlamydomonas cells

Parent chlamydomonas cells fuse to form a diploid embryo with four flagellae

The embryo secretes a hard, resistant coat that can survive drought and cold

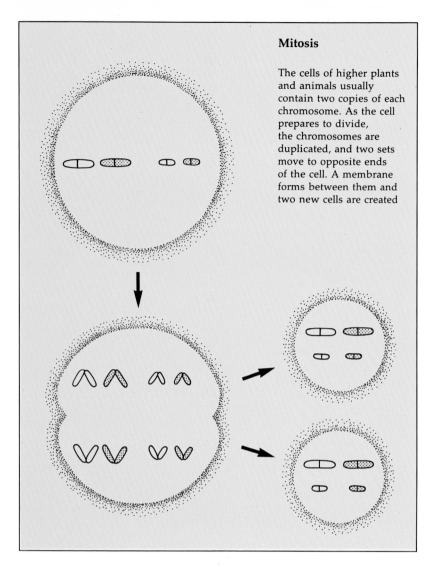

Mitosis

The cells of higher plants and animals usually contain two copies of each chromosome. As the cell prepares to divide, the chromosomes are duplicated, and two sets move to opposite ends of the cell. A membrane forms between them and two new cells are created

called a diploid, from the Greek word for double, because it has two copies of each chromosome, one from each parent. The nuclei soon separate again, but first the DNA is shuffled between them, so that each daughter cell receives an assortment of the parental genes.

This sort of cell division in which the two daughter cells share the chromosomes, taking one of each pair, is called meiosis. It occurs at some stage in the life-cycle of all creatures that reproduce sexually. In fact, without meiosis, sexual reproduction as we know it would be impossible. If cells kept mixing their genes by fusing with each other, each generation would have twice as much DNA as the last and there would soon be no room in the cell for anything else. Fusion cannot go on for ever and meiosis is the essential step which allows the diploid cell to shuffle its genes and distribute them equally between each of its daughters. It is the revolutionary step which made the evolution of sex a possibility; without sex there would be no birdsong, but without meiosis there would be no sex.

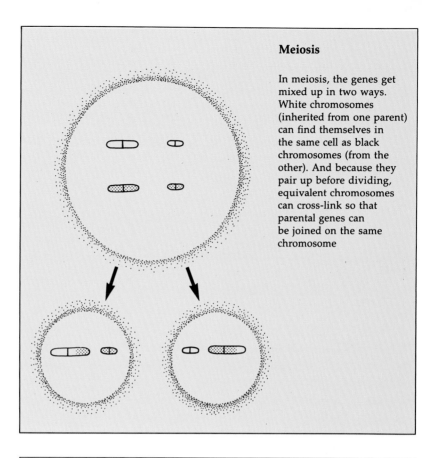

Meiosis

In meiosis, the genes get mixed up in two ways. White chromosomes (inherited from one parent) can find themselves in the same cell as black chromosomes (from the other). And because they pair up before dividing, equivalent chromosomes can cross-link so that parental genes can be joined on the same chromosome

The two types of cell division

There is a maximum size for cells, so as an organism grows it must divide in order to prevent its cells from growing too big. As cells divide, the genetic material must first copy itself exactly and send one copy to each of the two new cells. Bacteria have their library of genetic material stored on a single strand of DNA, but in more complex cells there are several strands of DNA called chromosomes. During the growth of the cell the DNA replicates so that each chromosome consists of two 'sister chromatids', and these are pulled apart as the cell divides. This normal type of cell division is called mitosis.

In a diploid cell, there are two copies of each chromosome. In meiosis, these chromosomes do not replicate as they do in mitosis, but instead, as the cell divides, each of the daughters receives one set. Genes become mixed in two ways. Chromosomes from both parents may end up in the same daughter cell, since the distribution of each half of the pair is at random. And chromosomes can crosslink so that daughter chromosomes may contain sections from each parent. The daughter cells produced by meiosis only contain a single set of chromosomes and are called 'haploid', which is Greek for single.

Sex and Changing Circumstances

In November 1963, to the hissing of sea-water and the considerable surprise of a boatload of local fishermen, Surtsey poked its head above the Atlantic waves. The belching smoke and boiling sea heralded the new volcano which soon formed a small island, a square kilometre of sterile grey lava and volcanic ash. Yet within five years, the tiny green alga *Chlamydomonas reinhardti* and six other chlamydomonas species had begun to make a home in pools of rainwater trapped in the lava.

Normally the cells of simple algae like chlamydomonas would be unable to survive a journey to the island, which lies over 40 kilometres (25 miles) south-west of Iceland. They need constant moisture and a food supply in order to live, and if drought or starvation failed to kill them the salt water soon would. However, chlamydomonas combines sexual reproduction with the creation of a resilient resting cell, capable of sitting out trouble or dispersing to new territory. The embryo formed by the fusion of the two parent cells differs from them not only by having two sets of chromosomes; it also differs in the details of its physical structure. When two chlamydomonas cells fuse, the embryo secretes a thick spiky cell wall and accumulates large quantities of starch. Protected by the cell wall and with enough food for many months, it may even be lifted onto the wind with the dust from a dry lake bed and deposited many miles away.

The chlamydomonas embryo that found itself on the barren lava flows of Surtsey got quite a shock, for its new environment was very different from its parents' home, probably a quiet pond in a farmer's field. But the new chlamydomonas cells which grew from it were the result of sexual reproduction, and so different from their parents; though none of the parental strains might have been able to survive the change, one of the offspring must have contained a combination of genes that allowed it to grow and reproduce.

The advantage of reproducing sexually when an organism must meet a new environment is so great that the strategy has been adopted by most higher plants and animals. Exactly how sexual reproduction evolved, we may never know for sure, but one interesting idea is that it might have started through individual cells eating each other. Before the mechanism for copying the genetic material became as sophisticated and reliable as it is in present organisms, acquiring a new set of chromosomes in this way would be an enormous help to any creature whose own genetic material was full of copying errors. However, this is only a guess, since many of the steps in the evolution of sex were taken a thousand million years ago and they left little record of themselves. Unfortunately sex does not fossilize well. In the same way that amoebae show how a life without sex is possible, examples from other groups of animals can provide hints about the sort of changes that might have led to the beautiful diversity of life that surrounds us today. One such group contains the sponges: odd creatures, so different from other animals that it is easy to believe they are trapped in a time warp.

OPPOSITE *Surtsey: an island appears above the waves.*

OPPOSITE Sponges are strange and often beautiful creatures, in many ways quite unlike other animals. Yet like most animals and plants they reproduce sexually in order to disperse.

Sponges can grow to a considerable size, forming cushions on the sea bed that are several feet across. A sponge feeds by drawing a current of sea-water through tiny pores in its body and filtering out any solid particles, before expelling the water through a larger vent. Some sponges produce a soft, flexible layer of spongin around themselves that supports them. (When the cells themselves have been killed and washed away, this is the part that is good for washing with.) Others support themselves with structures of chalk or silica, creating intricate and often beautiful skeletons.

Sponges reproduce in several ways. Some marine species can produce stalked buds that break away from the parent sponge and drift in the currents. If they settle in a suitable spot they grow into new sponges. Slightly more elaborate is the production of 'gemmules', small masses of cells enclosed in a protective capsule, that are produced by freshwater sponges and allow the animal to survive through the winter.

RIGHT A water flea gives birth to live young.

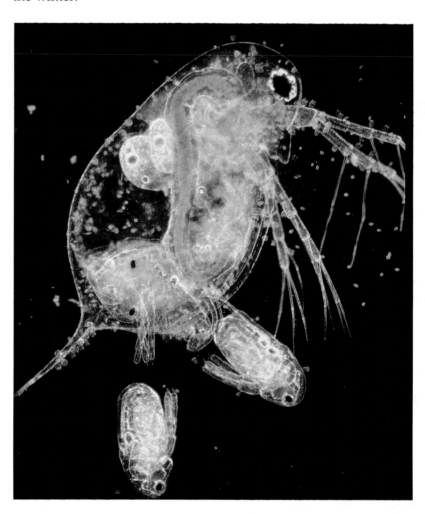

Such methods allow the sponge to reproduce asexually since both the buds and the gemmules are simply the result of normal cell division. Sponges can also reproduce sexually, producing sperm which are sucked in through the breathing pores and trapped by the feeding tissue before finding their way to nearby eggs. These fertilized eggs develop into free-swimming embryos, responsible, not for survival in the same place at a later date, but for dispersal to new habitats.

More complex plants and animals follow the same pattern. The water flea, daphnia, reproduces asexually throughout the summer, giving birth to live young that are all female and exact replicas of itself. As its numbers increase and its pond becomes crowded, the animals begin to produce males. These males mate with their sisters who then lay fertilized, drought-resistant eggs capable of withstanding a journey to a new pond stuck to the leg or bill of a passing bird, or of overwintering in the mud and hatching next spring to begin a new sexual generation. Either way, the threat of an uncertain future produces the same response: sex.

This combination of sexual and asexual reproduction crops up in all sorts of plants and animals. Asexual reproduction is widespread among flowering plants. Strawberries and creeping buttercup throw out long 'runners' which root themselves and then grow into new plants, identical in every way to their parents. Garlic reproduces itself with bulbs and the underground stems of bindweed are the gardener's curse because they are such an effective means of asexual propogation. All these asexual tricks allow a plant to spread locally, but in each case, when the time comes to invade new territory, these plants reproduce sexually and form seeds.

The change to sexual reproduction for the invasion of new territory is successful for the same reason in all these examples. The new territory is unpredictable, so the production of a variety of new forms increases the chances that some of the parents' progeny will survive. What confuses the picture is trying to sort out which bit of the life-cycle is which. In chlamydomonas cells there is only one set of chromosomes that joins with a second set to form the embryo, and this then divides without copying the chromosomes so that the cell is restored immediately to its original complement of genetic material, with one set of chromosomes per cell. Between the invention of simple sex and the appearance of sponges, some important changes have taken place. The body of the sponge is made up of diploid cells, which each have two sets of chromosomes. The same is true of all other higher plants and animals. These diploid organisms have grown from an embryo without any reduction division. The haploid cells, with a single set of chromosomes (which in chlamydomonas were the cells of the adult form) are now specialized sex cells, eggs and sperm (or, collectively, gametes) produced only in order to shuffle the genetic material. Yet in the sense that sexual reproduction prepares the offspring for an unpredictable environment, the system is the same as it was in chlamydomonas. The haploid cells still join together to form an embryo that will be dispersing to a new and unpredictable situation, for the embryo sponge leaves the parent and swims on its own before settling and beginning to grow into a new adult. What has changed is the stage in the life-cycle at which most of the growth occurs. In the green alga chlamydomonas, it was the haploids that turned the waters green, but the sponge colonies in rivers that feed on chlamydomonas are made up of diploid cells.

In *Chlamydomonas reinhardti*, sex cells are identical in appearance. In sponges, as in almost all higher plants and animals, there are two types of sex cell: a male cell, the sperm which is small and mobile, and a large, stationary female cell, the egg. It is this aspect of sex, maleness and femaleness, that is discussed in chapter two.

The Theory of Evolution

Darwin's idea that men might have descended from ape-like ancestors made him an easy target for the popular Press of his time, but what really annoyed the intellectuals of Victorian England was a deeper and more disturbing insight. Darwin had challenged the idea that life was created perfect; worse, he had suggested that it evolved through the interplay of fate and fortune.

The vast time-span of life on earth, the slow pace of evolutionary change, and the decisive part played by chance mutation, combined to make Darwin's ideas difficult to grasp. Yet the theory itself is simple and based on two observations. Firstly, not all animals and plants of the same species are identical. They might be taller, fatter, greener, braver or faster than others of the same species; in fact any two plants or animals will almost certainly be different in some way unless they are identical twins. Secondly, all animals and plants usually produce more offspring than will survive to breed. This means that many offspring must die before reaching maturity, and although some of these deaths will be accidental, death will tend to wipe out those creatures least well suited to their environment. If a species needs speed to escape from predators, the slowest animals will disappear. Where it is better to be slow and save energy, animals like the sloth will evolve to fill the niche, and fast-moving competitors will be unable to survive.

Linking these two facts provided the foundation for Darwin's theory. Darwin realized that nature produced a variety of individuals within each species, and that only some survived to pass on their characteristics to their offspring. A cycle of overproduction, death of the least suitable varieties, and the transmission of the best mutations to the next generation provided all that was necessary for evolution to occur. This theory of Natural Selection allowed Darwin to fit a great mass of previously unconnected observations into a coherent pattern, still today the main unifying idea in biology (although still with its rational critics).

During the years since its inception, Darwin's theory of evolution has itself undergone many changes. Like his predecessor Jean Baptiste

OPPOSITE *One of the more unlikely evolutionary success stories, the three-toed sloth is one of the commonest large mammals in the rainforests of South America. By slowing everything down, and keeping its body temperature close to the temperature of the outside world, the sloth lives on about a third of the energy required by other, similar-sized animals. This allows it to survive on a very poor-quality diet.*

Lamarck (the self-taught French zoologist whose misfortune it is to be remembered for his mistakes), Darwin believed that an animal changed during the course of its life, and that these changes might be passed on to its offspring. For Darwin this was just one of several mechanisms through which change could occur, and not central to his theory. But for Lamarck the inheritance of acquired changes, achieved by animals and plants striving to better themselves, was the essence of his evolutionary ideas. The next generation could then start from where the previous one had left off. An animal that constantly needed to extend its neck to reach the leaves of trees would leave offspring with longer necks, capable of reaching higher trees; and an animal that found itself constantly running away from predators would leave young that were faster.

Now that scientists understand the workings of simple cells a little better, it is difficult to see how experiences collected during a creature's life could be passed on to its offspring, since reading the genetic code seems to be a one-way process. A cell can correct mistakes in copying the DNA, but it cannot deliberately alter a gene in order to produce a new sort of protein. Nowadays, the accepted wisdom is that variety is the result of chance mutation, not a consequence of the use or disuse of a particular organ. But these insights have not destroyed Darwin's basic thesis: that evolution is the result of selection acting on a varied population.

What makes Darwin such a remarkable figure is that having spent five years struggling around the world on HMS *Beagle* and another twenty years preparing and writing *The Origin of Species* in which he set out these ideas, he went on to produce another blockbuster. In *The Origin of Species* Darwin argued that creatures best fitted to their environment were most likely to survive, but he also realized that survival was useless unless these creatures also reproduced. They could increase their numbers of offspring either by surviving longer or by putting more effort into reproduction. However, Darwin saw that the requirements of survival and the demands of sex often opposed each other and in his next epic, *The Descent of Man and Selection in Relation to Sex*, he extended the idea, briefly discussed in the earlier work, that animals might develop their often outrageous shapes and colours in order to persuade members of the other sex to mate. Only in this way could he explain the elaborate displays like the tail of the peacock. As we shall see in later chapters, the argument that he began over a hundred years ago is yet to be resolved.

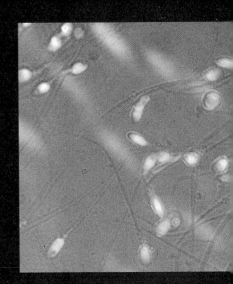

The eggs of a mosquito float on the surface of a pond (*below*). Like the eggs of all animals they are rich in food for the embryo and expensive to produce. In all animals, eggs are much larger than sperm (*right*). Most male animals produce thousands, even millions of sperm, which contain little more than genetic material. As we shall see, this simple difference between males and females is indirectly responsible for all the other differences between the sexes.

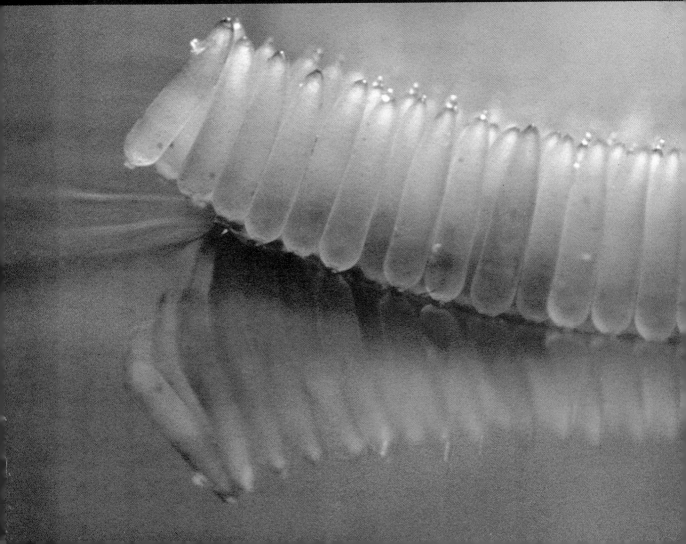

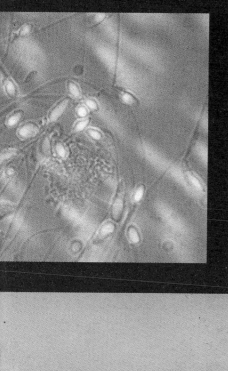

chapter two

From Sperm to Egg

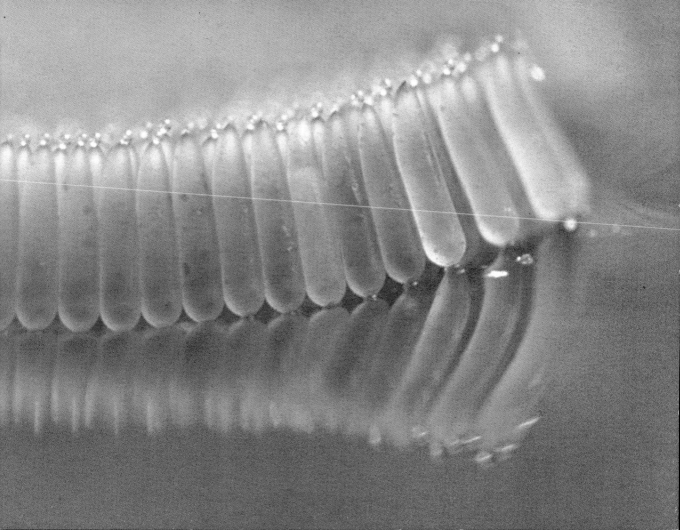

Male and Female

Again and again the difference between male and female is used as a metaphor to illuminate areas of life that are completely unconnected with sex. In fact the difference between male and female seems so important that around this dichotomy, whole schools of philosophy have attempted to structure a coherent picture of the universe. Opposing or complementary ideas almost invariably become associated with one of the sexes; the sun, iron and bombs are all male, while the moon, the earth, ships, cars and Mother Nature herself are all female. Yet however important the differences, male and female are not fundamental to the process of sex. Chlamydomonas manages sexual reproduction between two identical cells, while sexual reproduction in the common split-gill fungus (*Schizophyllum commune*) involves not two but 400,000 different mating types, and a very complicated set of rules about who can mate with whom. Nonetheless, most of the familiar creatures on the planet have only two sexes, and while this is not an immediate result of the sexual process, it is an important step in the evolution of sexual reproduction.

Biologically, the essential difference between male and female is that the females produce eggs which are comparatively large and immobile, while males produce smaller gametes (sperm) which can move. Each has a different role to play. The larger eggs contain more food reserves, which means that they will live longer and stand a correspondingly better chance of being fertilized, and the embryo they form will have more food reserves early in its life. In organisms with two distinct sexes, the female gametes always contribute more to the embryo than the males. In a sense the sperm are parasitic on the egg and rely on it for food. Mobile gametes, on the other hand, increase their chances of meeting a partner not by surviving longer in time, but by travelling further in space. For this they must be small and light. Gametes at each end of the size range are at an advantage while middle-sized gametes would be sitting on an unstable fence.

Males and females do not just make different types of gametes, they also generate vastly different numbers of them. Males produce thousands, often millions of sperm. Every time a bull mates it produces enough sperm to fertilize five billion cows, but usually only one of these sperm ever manages to fertilize anything, because cows, like most females, produce only relatively small numbers of eggs. There is no obvious need for such extraordinary overproduction, since there are a few mites and insects that reproduce quite satisfactorily by transferring less than two sperm for each egg. But these are exceptions and in most animals enormous numbers of sperm are wasted. How can such a system prosper if natural selection really does ensure that only the fittest, most efficient offspring survive? Part of the answer is that the more sperm a male produces, the better his chances of fertilizing at least some of the eggs of a female. This is only part of the story, however, for since males produce many more gametes than females, and mate repeatedly, one male can fertilize many females. So why

Women, like all female mammals, have two X chromosomes, and so all mammalian eggs contain a single X chromosome. In males, the sex chromosomes do not match, and sperm contain either an X or a Y chromosome. In birds, the male cells contain a matching pair of sex chromosomes, while in many insects the male has only one sex chromosome and the sperm receive either this or nothing at all. In all cases, the arrangement produces male and female offspring in equal numbers.

The extended trunk of a female green bonellia (Bonellia viridis). See page 35.

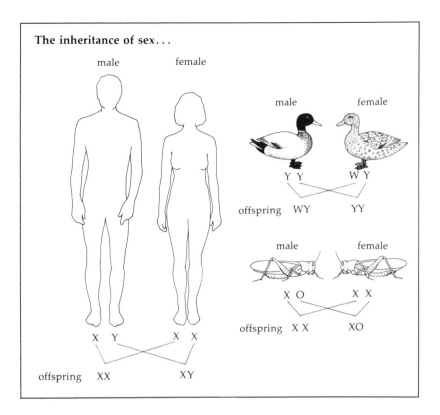

The inheritance of sex...

male   female

X   Y   X   X

offspring   XX   XY

male   female

Y   Y   W   Y

offspring   WY   YY

male   female

X   O   X   X

offspring   X X   XO

waste so much energy on males? Why not have more females than males instead of the normal equality?

The explanation of this apparent paradox is actually very simple. Successful males can fertilize many females, and since nature selects the fittest individuals, it will be these males that father most of the next generation. The overproduction of sperm may be wasteful for the species as a whole, but what is good for the species may not be the best of the individual. This is most easily illustrated with an example.

Red deer stags smash each other half to death in order to establish and maintain a harem. The biggest, most aggressive stags achieve most opportunities to mate with females, and about half of the stags father no fawns at all. Now if deer reproduced 'for the good of the species', we would expect the does to bear two female fawns for every male, and the stags would then have no cause to fight. In the next generation there would be enough does for everyone. But natural selection works on individuals, not on the whole species at once. A female red deer can produce only one fawn in a season, but while a daughter may only give birth five or six times in her life, a successful son may father twenty or thirty fawns and his eventual success will make up for the failure of his less fortunate brothers. On balance, the best strategy that an individual can pursue is to be the parent of equal numbers of males and females, a generalization that is true not only for deer, but for most sexually reproducing species.

The equal number of males and females is maintained from generation to generation by the way in which sex is determined. Like eye colour and blood type, an animal's sex is dictated by the information stored in its chromosomes. In men, the forty-eight chromosomes can be grouped as twenty-two matching pairs and two odd pieces that do not match. Because of their shape, they are called X and Y chromosomes. Women have no Y chromosome but two X's instead, so it is clear that these chromosomes have something to do with sex.

Sperm are produced by meiosis of male germ cells, and so for every sperm that receives an X, there is one with a Y chromosome. Meanwhile in the ovary, all the eggs must receive twenty-two non-sex chromosomes and one X chromosome, since X chromosomes are all the female has to give. When the egg and sperm fuse, half of the embryos are genetically male (XY) and half are female (XX) and the equal ratio of males to females is maintained.

The genetic mechanism of sex determination is the same in all mammals. It is also the same in most plants which bear male and female flowers on different individuals. But it is far from universal. In birds, reptiles and fishes the male carries the matching chromosomes and it is the female that has the odd one. In many insects there is no Y chromosome at all; males simply have one less chromosome than females.

All these methods of sex determination seem designed to ensure that equal numbers of male and female offspring are produced. In practice however, there is a slight bias towards one sex or the other. This is because there are many ways in which the ratio of males to females can be changed during and after conception. If for instance male fetuses abort more frequently than females, or young females are more accident prone than males, there will be more of one sex than the other in the adult population. This sort of secondary determination of the sex ratio is common in many animals. In deer, stress during pregnancy is more likely to cause the abortion of a male fetus than of a female one. This certainly makes sense for the doe; a male fawn born of a stressful pregnancy will be weak. Because males must grow faster than females, twice as many stags as does die in their first winter. A weak male fawn is unlikely to grow into a dominant stag capable of holding a large harem, but a weak doe may well survive to mate and produce offspring.

Despite the increased abortion rate for male fetuses, there are normally equal numbers of male and female fawns born in spring. The abortion of males is balanced by more conceptions of male than female offspring: weak does tend to abort male fawns, but strong does are rather more likely to produce males than females.

While the rule for most animals is that there will be roughly equal numbers of males and females, there are exceptions. The queen honeybee produces all female offspring for most of the season, and a few males towards the end of the year. Male bees, the drones, are produced from unfertilized eggs, whereas females (the workers and queens) develop from the fertilized eggs and the queen has complete control over the sex of her offspring. In other animals, turtles and crocodiles, for example, the ratio of males to females is determined by the temperature at which the eggs develop.

A totally different mechanism for determining sex is found in the green bonellia (*Bonellia viridis*), a strange marine creature belonging to a little-known group of animals, the Echiurans. This animal is remarkable not only for the way in which an individual's sex is determined, but also for the thousandfold difference in size between the males and females. Female bonellias live with their bodies wedged into clefts between rocks around the Mediterranean coast. Protruding from the cleft is an enormous trunk, up to a metre long, with which the female animal gathers food and males. The males of this species, however, are only a millimetre long. They move down the trunk of the female, through her mouth and into her gullet, and then bore through into her genital tract where they fertilize her eggs. The larvae produced are of indeterminate sex. If they settle on a rock, they develop as females and grow their enormous trunks, but should they settle on a female's trunk, the larvae develop within a few days into males.

Slightly less extreme is the difference in size between female angler fishes and their mates, whose lives are passed as parasites attached to the body of the female. Predators in the black depths of the oceans probably meet only occasionally, since there are few of them and vast spaces to hide in. The males' parasitic lifestyle ensures that the female has an available partner when she needs one and that infrequent chance meetings are not wasted simply because she is not carrying ripe eggs at the time.

LEFT A female angler fish with her collection of parasitic males.

Differences between males and females may have nothing to do with their sexual roles. Instead they may simply help the male and female to exploit slightly different foods and so avoid unnecessary competition with each other. Even very slight, apparently insignificant differences may be important. The male goldfinch, for example, can reach the seeds of the teazle which lie at the bottom of long spiked tubes. The beaks of females are shorter by about a millimetre and they feed instead on betony or scrophularia. To feed on teazle (which the females will attempt if kept in captivity), they must turn down the spikes with their beaks before pulling the seeds out. A similar explanation has been suggested for the difference in size between male and female birds of prey. In most animals the male is the larger of the two sexes, a difference easily explained for animals like the red deer, in which the males must compete for access to females. Among birds of prey, however, it is usually the female which is the larger of the two. The male peregrine is about a third lighter than the female, and the male sparrowhawk only half the weight of his mate, and because of this each bird will specialize in feeding on different prey. The female sparrowhawk, for example, can tackle a fully grown wood pigeon, a task quite beyond the male. Unable to kill large prey, the male hunts blue tits and finches, and the two birds do not normally compete with each other for food.

Although the essential biological difference betwen males and females is the type of gamete which each produces, we normally use other characteristics to distinguish between them. While some of these can be explained as adaptations to different feeding behaviours, the stag's antlers, the lion's mane and the cock's comb serve a different purpose, much more closely linked with the sexual process. Before we can understand why it is the males and not the females that usually carry these strange distinguishing features, we must look a little harder at the differences between sperm and eggs.

The Attraction of Sperm

To cut a biologist down to size, collect a good pile of microscope slides smeared with sperm from different animals and get your victim to try and identify the fathers. It is easy enough to identify sperm, but fiendishly difficult to tell what species it comes from. The sperm of sea urchins, shrews and elephant seals are almost identical. Even the sperm from an elephant seal and a moss are not dissimilar: both are elegantly streamlined and propelled along by thrashing tails. Both contain a batch of genetic material, a store of readily available energy, and nothing else. These two you can actually tell apart, because the moss sperm have two tails and the elephant seal sperm only one, but considering the differences between the parents, the similarity is still remarkable. This almost uniform design is one consequence of sexual inequality. As males become specialized to produce more and more sperm, the pressure mounts. The race to the egg becomes a race for survival, and the sperm are built for speed. All extra weight has been shed, all unnecessary equipment left behind.

Beyond this first stage of sophistication there are many more ways in which sperm can improve their chances. One is by developing a method for finding an egg rather than simply bumping into it. A sperm able to 'taste' the presence of an egg could in theory beat the competition simply by swimming in circles once it detected its target. This would keep the sperm close to the egg, and their chances of bumping into each other would be much improved. Better still, if a sperm could detect changes in the concentration of egg-chemicals and could swim towards ever higher concentrations, it would then have a built-in homing device. Mosses and liverworts have evolved just such a system.

The sexual parts of mosses are carried on the tips of the leafy shoots, surrounded by fine hairs which trap and hold a film of water. The sperm are contained in thin-walled sacs, and when the sac is wetted, the ripe sperm are released to swim away. They may be helped on their journey by passing insects, or splashed about in the rain, for although they may swim for five or six hours, they cannot travel far

BELOW The brook liverwort (Marchantia polymorpha), which often grows unexpectedly in well-watered flower pots. The eggs grow in rows beneath the ribs of the umbrella-shaped supports.

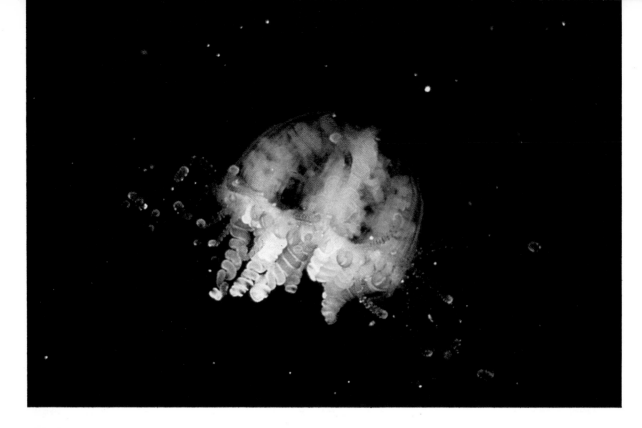

under their own steam. Always, at the last stage of the journey, their random movement becomes directional, and across the last few millimetres they swim straight towards the egg.

ABOVE *A hydrozoan jellyfish, one of the few animals in which chemicals released by the eggs have been shown to attract sperm.*

The eggs of mosses grow at the bottom of a flask-shaped container, carried at the tip of a leafy green shoot. The neck of the flask is blocked by a plug of cells and when the egg matures, this plug explodes outwards splattering the surrounding area with ruptured cells and their sugary contents. As the sperm sense the presence of the sugar, they turn towards its source.

Sugar is probably the only cue that moss sperm use in their search for eggs, but other plants send out more distinctive signals. By producing a chemical that attracts only closely related sperm, the brown seaweed *Fucus serratus* (the bladder wrack of rocky shores and amateur meteorologists) avoids the traffic jams and confusion that might be caused if its eggs were to attract every sperm in the vicinity. In flowering plants, the production of sperm is more complex and it is the pollen tube which is chemically guided on its way to the ovary. So it is surprising to find that by contrast, the chemical attraction of sperm to eggs has been demonstrated in only a few animals. Most of these are pretty obscure sea creatures, like the hydroid *Hydractinia echinata* which lives on the backs of shells inhabited by hermit crabs. Of the more familiar animals, only a few jellyfish have been found to release sperm attractants. These are active only on sperm from animals of the same species and so form part of the mechanism that prevents the formation of infertile hybrids. However, the sperm and eggs of most animals simply bump into each other by chance.

The Birth of Copulation

The adventure that first took animals from their life on water to life on land must have been slow and difficult. Quite apart from inventing ways for moving around out of water and breathing air, animals could never become completely independent of the seas and rivers without developing some method for fertilizing their eggs which did not involve the sperm swimming through water. Without such a change, all animals would have to return to the water to mate, as most frogs and toads still do.

The first breakthrough that made sex on land a possibility was the

During courtship the male cuttlefish (Sepia officinalis) displays a shifting zebra-striped pattern to the female by expanding and contracting colour cells on his skin. Cuttlefish are members of the squid family and swarms gather for communal courtship. When they eventually copulate the male uses a specially modified arm called the hectocotylus to insert a sperm package into the mantle of the female. The hectocotylus of the closely related paper nautilus becomes detached from the male during or even prior to copulation, and the whole structure is left attached to the female.

39

development of the spermatophore. Spermatophores are packets of sperm, wrapped tightly in a bag of some sort, which prevents the sperm from drying out before they are taken into the genital tract of the female. While some sort of protection for sperm is essential if animals are to mate on land, the reason why spermatophores developed in the ancestors of land animals remains a mystery. Perhaps it was to help transfer the sperm between males and females that had already developed internal fertilization. Octopuses still transfer their sperm in this way, males of the giant octopus (*Octopus dofleini*) pushing a metre-long sperm sac into the genital passage of the female. Perhaps, as still occurs in some crabs, the spermatophore was stuck onto a female so that she carried it around as a sperm store until she was ready to lay her eggs. We may never know, because once animals began to use spermatophores to reproduce on land, so many new

Houseflies copulating in mid-air.

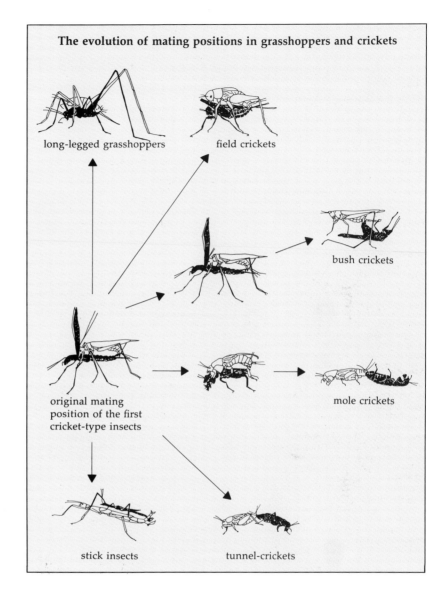

The evolution of mating positions in grasshoppers and crickets

long-legged grasshoppers

field crickets

bush crickets

mole crickets

original mating
position of the first
cricket-type insects

stick insects

tunnel-crickets

*The distant ancestors of crickets probably passed spermatophores from
male to female by first depositing them on the ground, as scorpions do
today. The genital opening of the female would have been beneath her
body, so the first crickets that transferred their spermatophore directly
probably mated with the female (shown above in white) on top of the male.
In the course of evolution, things have changed. In some species, the
female remains on top of the male throughout copulation, as in the long
legged grasshoppers and field crickets. Bush and mole crickets begin
copulating in this way, but the male may then change position. Tunnel
crickets have lost the female on top position altogether, and begin
copulating end to end. In mantids and stick insects, the male is on top, but
must now twist his abdomen beneath the female to reach her genital
opening.*

Barnacles cannot move, but the male nonetheless fertilizes the female internally, introducing his extraordinarily long penis into her mantle cavity. Consequently barnacles must live in dense clusters if they are to mate.

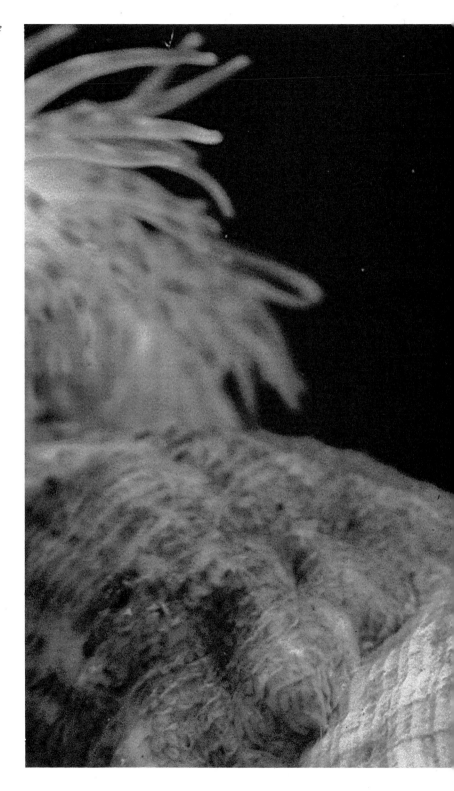

possibilities opened up that evolution quickly brought about substantial changes in the practice of internal fertilization. The brook salamander today transfers his spermatophores to the female by pressing his vent against hers and attempting to pass them directly into her vaginal cavity. Success is not guaranteed and if the sperm sac misses its mark, the male will press it home with his hind feet. The scorpion's mode of transfer is more subtle: the male deposits a packet of sperm on to the ground. His claws gripping the female's, he draws her over it and she stoops to collect it in her genital opening. Crickets possess an unusual sperm sac that does part of the male's job. Only the neck is inserted into the vagina of the female, and the main body of the sac remains outside. As the sac dries out it contracts, forcing the sperm down the neck and into the vagina.

The springtails have made a different use of their sperm sacs. Springtails are much simpler insects even than crickets. They have no wings and when disturbed they leap by flicking down a special springing organ that is folded beneath their body, which gives them their name. The springtails are often described as primitive or relic insects, but their mating has evolved so that the male and female no longer need to meet. The spermatophore of these insects is in fact only a drop of sperm on a thin stalk, protected from complete desiccation by a skin that forms over its surface as it dries. The males leave hundreds of these lying around on the ground. As a female walks across one, her moist genital cavity wets the surface of the sac and frees the sperm, which quickly swim through the vagina to the eggs.

Spiders have evolved along a different path and although they have lost their sperm sacs, they still transfer sperm indirectly. A male spider spins a small triangular pad of silk to collect his sperm, which is ejected from the genital pore on the underside of his abdomen. He then sucks this drop into the hollow tip of his palps, the extra limbs that lie close to his mouth, rather like a doctor filling a hypodermic syringe. To inseminate the female, he must thrust his pedipalp into her genital opening and inject his sperm.

Much more straightforward is the use of a copulatory organ to introduce the sperm directly from the testes of the male into the vaginal cavity of the female. The penis of mammals is of course the most familiar of these organs, but it is not unique. Snakes and lizards have two penes, either of which can be used in copulation. The sharks and rays practice internal fertilization, but in this group the male introduces his sperm with his fins. Each pelvic fin has a massive outgrowth, with a groove on the inner edge. To inseminate the female, he places these together to form a tube and forces them into the female's vent, passing his sperm down the hole between them. Only a few bony fishes, like the guppy, fertilize their eggs internally and these introduce sperm sacs into the female's vent with their modified anal fins.

Birds all copulate and fertilize their eggs internally. The shell which protects the egg from drying out during its incubation is impenetrable to sperm, and so like the eggs of reptiles, the eggs of birds must be fertilized before the shell is laid down. Drakes and ganders have a modified vent with large lips which the male can press into the female. Since this is not a true penis the ornithologists, running out of words, have dubbed it a phallus. However most birds possess no special copulatory organ and sperm is passed from male to female simply by pressing the vents together. Perhaps they simply cannot afford to carry all that extra weight around, so make do with the bare essentials. The true penis is peculiar to mammals and allows the male to deposit his sperm well inside the female.

All animals that have adopted internal fertilization can provide extra protection for their young by carefully concealing their eggs as they lay them, or surrounding them with an impermeable shell once they have been fertilized. Some reptiles and fishes keep the eggs inside their bodies until development is complete, and instead of laying eggs, they give birth to live young. Often, in such cases, the mother not only protects the developing embryo but feeds it as well. In most mammals, the embryo becomes attached to the uterus through the placenta, and oxygen and nutrients can be passed from the mother to her young. This system is very economical; the food that nourishes the growing embryo is only provided once the egg is fertilized, and the early stages of development have been completed.

Copulation has made possible the invasion of the land, while internal fertilization has allowed the extended protection of the young by the female. Plants have solved the same problems in different ways.

The simplest land plants, mosses, liverworts and lichens, still depend on a thin layer of water through which the sperm can swim to the egg. Even in the mosses and liverworts, the egg never leaves the parent plant, fertilization is internal and the developing embryo lives as a parasite on its mother. In flowering plants too, the egg remains protected by the parent, and after it has been fertilized, the mother plant may further contribute by providing food or protection to the growing seed. Land plants cannot go looking for mates and so of course they cannot copulate. As a result they have been forced to invent a rather different way of invading the land and other more subtle methods for improving their chances of fertilization.

Like animals that produce a spermatophore, flowering plants packet their sperm in a bag which prevents them from drying out. In this case the bag is a pollen grain. Whereas a spermatophore contains hundreds of sperm, the hard wall of the pollen grain surrounds only two. When a pollen grain lands on a suitable flower, it begins to grow, pushing a hollow tube into the tissues of the plant on which it has landed. As it goes, it feeds on sugars released by the female flower and is guided by chemicals in the surrounding tissue. The sperm remain trapped inside the pollen grain as it grows towards the egg, but they stay close to the growing tip so that when the tube reaches the ovum they have only a short journey ahead of them. Because of the peculiarities of plant eggs, both sperm are needed to fertilize the seed, one as the genetic father of the new plant and one to fertilize the seed's 'food nucleus'.

It is not difficult to believe that nature invented sex because it

The process of pollination

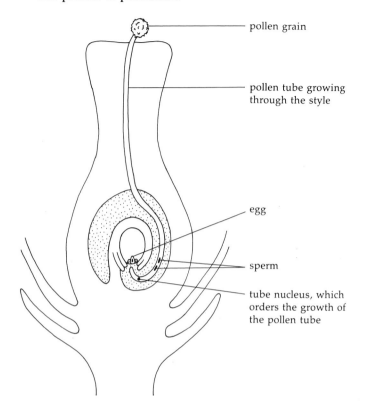

pollen grain

pollen tube growing
through the style

egg

sperm

tube nucleus, which
orders the growth of
the pollen tube

seemed like a good idea at the time and only later began to appreciate the difficulties involved in bringing the gametes together. She has tried sperm attractants, which survive in the jellyfish; and she has experimented with copulation, using the cooperation of both parents to coordinate and sychronize their sexual activity. While this last innovation makes things easy for the gametes and has made possible a life independent of the water, it has created a whole new set of problems for the parents. If they want to reproduce they must first find each other, or at least, as in many flowering plants, find a messenger to carry their sperm.

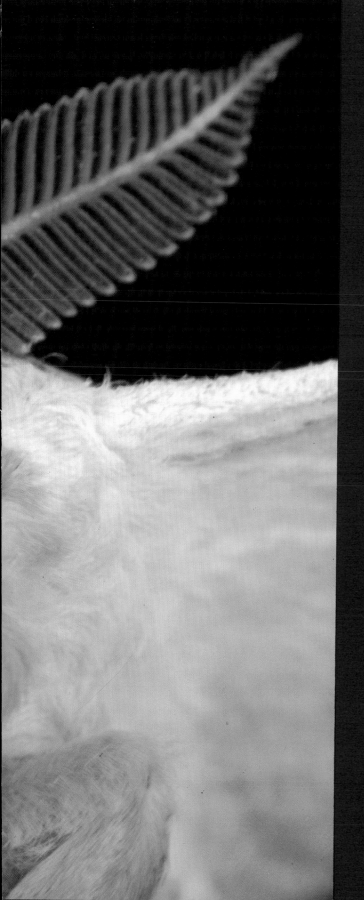

chapter three

Finding a Mate

The enormous antennae of the male
emperor moth can detect minute quantities
of chemicals released by the female.

The Search

Although many animals simply release their eggs and sperm to find each other as best they can, copulation is so widespread in the animal world that we take it almost for granted that most animals pair up, or at least come together in groups, before mating. Codfish form pairs, the male pressing his vent against the female and releasing his milt at exactly the same moment that she releases her eggs. Frogs use a similar technique, but the vents are held together by the male who clasps his mate from behind in the piggy back position that biologists call amplexus. In the Gulf of Mexico, the sea urchin *Tripneustes esculatus* disappears from the rock surfaces on which it is usually found and congregates beneath ledges in the shallows where the eggs and sperm will not be so diluted by the vast volume of sea water. Dog whelks aggregate before spawning, and even blue limpets pair up before shedding their gametes into the sea. While animals which fertilize their eggs externally sometimes pair together before mating, internal fertilization leaves the parents no choice. If they want to mate, they must first find a partner.

Copulation makes life very easy for gametes, but copulation has brought with it a new batch of complications because it has completely shifted the responsibility of searching for the opposite sex from the gametes to the adults. Since males and females both need each other, the process of finding a mate is usually cooperative. Often one sex will advertise itself and the other spends its time looking through the personal columns – listening for courtship songs, searching for a familiar pattern or sniffing the air for a tell-tale scent.

A successful male may attract many females and mate with all of them, but females often need to mate only once in order to fertilize all their eggs. So females do not stand to gain as much by conspicuously hawking their wares; on the contrary, they have everything to lose, since the process of advertising for a mate can also attract predators. Consequently it is usually the males that run the risk of performing the advertising displays.

Animals are very vulnerable during the act of mating because they are less able to escape from predators or defend themselves. Advertising for a mate can be even more dangerous, since predators can use the advertisement to find their prey. Mating swarms of mayflies are easy prey for swallows, and the frog-eating bat specializes at homing in on the mating call of frogs. There is a conflict between an animal's need to advertise for mates and the need to avoid detection by predators, and the gambits and countergambits in this conflict have generated many of the fascinating complexities and subtleties of mating behaviour. As predators specialize in locating prey, the prey may change its strategy for finding mates, perhaps by switching from one signalling medium to another. Sight, sound and smell are the commonest means of communication between mates, and the one used will depend on the animals and the circumstances in which they are searching for each other.

Sight

Of all the senses, sight is the least suitable for finding a mate. In the dark depths of the ocean it is practically useless. Even in shallow water where light penetrates, it may be impossible to see through the soup of suspended silt and plankton. On land, sight is of limited use by night, and even in the daytime, mist or mirage can make it difficult to see properly. More importantly, light cannot travel round corners, so that in tall grassland, scrub or woodland, animals may only be a few feet apart but unable to see each other.

Creatures that go out looking for mates are effectively restricted to a few habitats where clear vision is guaranteed. Zebra spiders, for example, live on rocks and walls where there is little or no cover, and their exceptional eyesight is used for mate-finding as well as for hunting. Many grasshoppers will jump on anything which looks like a female, and for some this is their only way of finding a mate. Bare, sandy areas throughout the northern United States are often inhabited by the mottled sand grasshopper (*Spharagemon collare*). The males find a patch of open ground with a clear view and stand inconspicuously in the centre. Anything that moves they approach, males and females alike, even completely unrelated species.

Such a lack of discrimination is quite common in insects, many of which can see movement and colour better than they can distinguish details of form. Unfortunately the tactic of jumping on anything that moves is risky, and beewolves (*Philanthus bicinctus*) for instance often pay a high price for their impetuosity.

The beewolves are a group of digger wasps which specialize in catching bumble-bees, the females using them as food for their developing larvae. Beewolves sting and paralyse the bees, then carry them off to a burrow, where they inter them in batches of two or three along with a single egg. When the egg hatches, the growing beewolf larva feeds on the bodies of the bumblebees.

During the mating season, the male beewolves stand on conspicuous perches and fly at almost anything that passes. Often they find a female beewolf this way, but sometimes they find themselves in the clutches of a robber-fly, a vicious hunter with keen eyesight which catches its prey on the wing. Flying straight towards it, the male beewolf must be one of its easiest catches – in fact if robber-flies had a sense of humour, they would certainly tell jokes about beewolves.

Later in the season, inquisitive flights by males can become even more risky. Once the female is mated, she loses all interest in sex and concentrates only on stocking burrows for her eggs. Unfortunately for the male beewolf, she does not restrict her attentions exclusively to bumble-bees. Male beewolves are often found paralysed in the burrows of the females, but other females are very rarely found. So the behaviour of beewolves once again underlines the point that it is the sex with the most to gain that takes most of the risks.

In species that attract their mates with some sort of eye-catching visual display, it is the performers that are most at risk, while now the

The zebra spider uses its remarkable eyes to search for potential mates. The large forward-facing eyes are particularly sophisticated, moving up, down and from side to side, and backwards and forwards for focussing. They can even be rotated slightly, a movement used to pinpoint prey and mates.

searchers can remain hidden. Consistent with the theory that it is the male who takes the risks, it is the males which put on the show. Mayfly males (*Ephemera danica*) attract females by dancing in swarms. Each flies a few feet into the air, parachutes gently down again, wings outstretched, then immediately begins to fly upwards once more. The dance may be repeated for hours on end, interrupted only by sudden gusts of wind or the appearance of a female. When a female flies through the swarm, the males grab her, often three or four hanging on to her at once. The mass of bodies flies awkwardly to the ground or on to a bush, where one of the males will eventually succeed in mating.

These displays, performed by thousands of males together, are obvious to predators as well as females, and mayflies are easy prey. During the week in which the mayflies emerge, the swallows, martins, and wagtails gorge themselves. But the mayfly's strategy is not without subtlety. Because the insects synchronize their breeding, they all emerge, mate and die during this one week in early spring and so they do not provide a reliable diet. Their predators eat well for a short while, but without a consistent supply of food throughout the summer, the birds cannot raise enough young each year to threaten the mayfly population. Although they are heavily preyed on, there is safety in numbers, since despite the carnage, the chance of any individual being eaten is small.

Cabbage white butterflies are on the wing throughout the summer, and so for these insects there is no safety in numbers. Yet still the males search for the flash of white that announces a possible mate, constantly exposing themselves to predators. Their protection is rather different – they taste disgusting. The caterpillars feed on plants which contain mustard oil and they store this in large quantities in their bodies. Birds soon learn that the conspicuous white butterflies are bad news and the males are left alone to search for their mates.

Closely related species like the small white butterfly are often not as distasteful as the large white, possibly because they specialize in feeding on the younger cabbage leaves and other plants that contain less of the distasteful oil. Obviously it is in the interests of these butterflies to imitate the appearance of the large white, for they will then be spared by birds unable to distinguish them. As we shall see later, having two species that are trying their best to look alike complicates the process of finding a mate.

Luminescence

While looking for a mate in daylight is risky and often rather ineffective, visual advertising in the dark paradoxically holds more promise of success. Night hunters usually rely on scent or sound to find their prey and may be unable to take advantage of eye-catching visual displays.

Many groups of animals, and even some fungi, are able to glow in the dark, but often the function of this luminescence is a mystery. It may serve to confuse predators, or help to set up territorial boundaries. The lights in the mouth of the hatchet fish seem the perfect lure

A female mayfly that flies into a swarm is immediately grabbed by males, often several at once. The swarm of males was dancing beside a hawthorn bush, which protected them from the wind and acted as a marker to attract the females. After a short and clumsy flight, the mating bundle shown here landed in a nearby barley field. The female is at the top, and below her is her mate, clasping her with the tip of his abdomen. At the bottom is a second, unsuccessful male.

for prey, attracting small fish like moths to a flame. So too does the luminous bait of the female angler-fish, dangling from a rod in front of her mouth; but in this case, the bait may also attract male angler-fish, whose eyes are very well developed despite being useless for catching prey in the complete blackness of the ocean depths. While many deep-sea fishes have light organs which may play a part in mate-finding, there may also be other uses for this eerie luminescence that are as yet unguessed at, for deep-sea fishes are almost impossible to study. However one species, the midshipman (*Porichthys notatus*), comes close inshore at spawning time and can be caught and kept in a normal aquarium. This of course tells us nothing about how the male and female find each other in the first place, but it has shown that the light organs play a role in courtship, the male flashing repeatedly when introduced to a glowing female.

Much more is known about the behaviour of fireflies and glow-worms, both of which are actually beetles and both of which attract their mates by luminescent signalling. The female glow-worm (*Lampyris noctiluca*) hangs from a suitable support and twists her body so that the luminous patch beneath her abdomen is aimed skyward. Males fly around searching for the females, and when they see a promising glow they fold their wings and plummet earthward with amazing accuracy, usually landing within inches of their target.

It is uncommon to find females taking the risk of conspicuous display, and fireflies, though related to glow-worms, adopt the more usual roles. Here it is the male that displays, usually by flashing a distinctive Morse code while in flight. For *Photinus macdermotti*, the code is two flashes, two seconds apart, followed by a gap. A female *P. macdermotti* seeing this, will answer with a single flash a second after the male's signal. The male watches for females returning his signal and lands close to the answering flash.

The system seems almost infallible. The fireflies signal at night when few flying predators are active that might spot their flashing. Once the male has found a female, they identify each other before approaching. But the male fireflies are not safe in spite of their elaborate precautions. The female of a different species of firefly, *Photuris versicolor*, mimics the answering flashes of the female *P. macdermotti*, luring the males to land beside her. Instead of finding a mate, the *P. macdermotti* male is jumped on and eaten, for the photuris fireflies are predators. There is no doubt that this misleading 'come-hither' is deliberate. The mating signal of the *P. versicolor* is three quick flashes delivered in about half a second, to be answered by a single flash from the female, a response quite different from that which she uses to lure her prey to its death. Only after mating does the female change her behaviour, responding not only to the flashes of *P. macdermotti* but to the flashes of other possible prey species as well. As a result the males of most fireflies have become very fussy, rejecting the invitations of any female whose signal is suspect.

Visual displays are easy to locate, and animals that attempt to catch the eye of their mates must have some protection from predators.

Many male fireflies signal in flight, but the Malaysian folded-wing firefly (Pteropteryx malaccae) attracts flying females from a perch in a tree.

While butterflies rely on toxins to protect them, and mayflies play a sort of Russian roulette with their predators, the fireflies have adopted a complex signalling method that identifies the partners to each other from a safe distance. Yet instead of ensuring complete safety, the messages are read, deciphered and exploited by other fireflies. As we shall see in the next section, sound is more difficult to locate, but the messages it carries are also easily deciphered.

Sound

Making a noise is a good way to attract attention, since like visual signals, sounds can carry subtle and distinctive messages. Calling for a mate also avoids some of the problems associated with visual advertising since sound travels round corners, and so a signal can be delivered from a safe hiding place and its author can attract a mate while escaping the attentions of predators. Furthermore, sounds can easily be modified to fit changing circumstances. An animal that calls loudly when well protected may call quietly when exposed, or even change its call completely in order to deceive its hunters. Animals that use sound to attract their mates often take advantage of all these aspects of the medium.

Of the animals that use sound to attract their mates, birds are the most familiar, and just as with animals which communicate to potential partners by sight, it is the male who most often takes the risk of advertising his whereabouts. The message in his song must explain that he wishes to mate and that he belongs to the right species. The experienced birdwatcher, like the birds, learns to identify species by

RIGHT The shy grasshopper warbler (Locustella naevia) takes its name from its clicking, almost mechanical song which like the sound of the true grasshoppers is almost impossible to pinpoint. As the bird turns his head, the sound grows louder and softer, making it even more difficult for predators to calculate how far away he is.

their calls even when they look much the same. Unfortunately this trick often only works in spring when the birds are looking for mates, and later in the year the poor birdwatcher is as confused as ever.

Once animals have evolved to use sound in their search for a partner, they might as well make as much noise as they can and so garden birds sing their heart out and foxes scream at full volume. Calls for attracting mates must be distinct from threat or alarm calls, since the male certainly cannot afford to give the wrong impression. Often the type of habitat in which the bird lives influences the type of call it makes, forest birds using low-pitched, monotonous songs that carry clearly through the trees.

Some animals have evolved their own built-in sound boxes to amplify the sound, like the enormous throat pouches of bullfrogs. Others use artificial means of amplification. The cricket *Gryllus integer* from the southern United States often sings from the entrance to cicada burrows. Cicadas spend much of their lives underground as larvae, and the burrow from which an adult has emerged is often several feet deep. This makes an ideal resonator for cricket song, as well as a safe retreat in case of emergency. Male mole crickets go one better and make their own burrows, acoustically designed to get the very best from their mating call. The burrow acts as a megaphone, so even humans can hear it almost half a mile away. Just as important, the burrows direct the sound upwards, so that the females can hear the song as they fly about looking for a mate.

Mole crickets may increase the volume of their calls by a third with this trick, but this is not much when compared with the performance of the chirping cricket *Oecanthus burmeisteri* from southern Africa. This smart beast gnaws neat, pear-shaped holes into leaves and sits at the narrow end, spreading his long wings to cover the rest of the hole. This creates a baffle, a concept that hi-fi enthusiasts may understand even if the cricket does not. All that is important for the cricket is that this boosts the volume of his song more than threefold.

The kakapo, the world's only flightless parrot, uses both natural and artificial amplification for its song. This strange bird was thought to be near extinction, but recently a new colony has been found in the thick beech forest on Stewart Island at the southern tip of New Zealand. It is no surprise that a nocturnal bird living in thick woodland uses sound to attract its mates, but almost everything else about the operation is quite unusual. The males puff themselves up until they are almost spherical, filling themselves with air to create a sound box. This they set resonating with a booming sound from their vocal cords, like the sound made by blowing across a bottle. To amplify the call even more they excavate a shallow bowl in the ground, in which they stand so that their call is reflected far and wide to echo across the forest.

Although animals that sing are more difficult for their enemies to locate than animals that display visually, their advertising often leads them into trouble. Of the animals that hunt by listening to the sound of their prey, perhaps the most formidable is the frog-eating bat. Its ears are carefully engineered to locate the direction and strength of

BELOW A male field cricket at the mouth of a cicada hole. The deep hole acts as a resonator, amplifying the cricket's song, and is also a safe retreat from cats and other large predators.

RIGHT *Frogs and toads amplify their calls by stretching their throats to create a resonant sound box.*

BELOW *Frogs in amplexus. A successful male holds a female common frog (Rana temporaria), waiting for her to shed her eggs.*

In Central America, the mating call of male frogs attracts unwelcome attention from frog-eating bats.

sound, and although the bat's echo-location system is designed to operate at very high frequencies, the frog-eating bat has been able to adapt to locating the sounds of potential prey. A native of central American jungles, the frog-eating bat homes in on the sound of calling frogs, but is quite unable to detect frogs that sit quietly. It can distinguish the calls of edible from those of poisonous frogs. Even frogs that are too big for it to eat are ignored, identified by their deep croaks, and left in peace. Once it locates a suitable frog, the bat swoops down and grabs it with its teeth.

To avoid the danger posed by the bats, the frogs have developed some neat tricks of their own. One of the frogs on which the bats prey is the pug-nosed tree-frog. On moonlit nights, when the tree-frog can see the bats coming, it will perch on conspicuous rocks and use loud calls which the females can easily locate. If a bat attacks, the frog sees it coming and jumps into the stream, or hops beneath a bush. But on dark nights the frogs hide beneath leaves and use a simple whining call. There are no sharp clicks in this call, and both bats and female frogs find it more difficult to locate. The frogs also call less often, and so on dark nights, fewer males find females. The risk of being eaten outweighs the benefits likely to come from more conspicuous advertising for a mate.

This predator-avoidance technique has been taken a step further by the Texas field cricket *Gryllus integer*. The louder they call, the more mates they attract. Although this sounds like a prescription for every male to sing his heart out, that is not what happens. Some males do not call at all. Instead they position themselves near to a calling male and do their best to intercept females that are trying to find the source of the sound. They are not always successful and they mate less often than the calling males. Yet despite this poor reproductive performance, the behaviour survives from generation to generation, so the disadvantage of attracting less females must have some compensation. The advantage that the crickets gain by remaining silent is that they avoid the attentions of a small, parasitic fly. Although the fly does not have the sophisticated hearing of a bat, its single sound-sensitive membrane can locate a singing cricket. On warm nights, female flies move in on the singing male crickets and spray them with their larvae. These burrow into the cricket and within a few weeks the cricket is dead. Non-calling males of course suffer much less. They may not mate as frequently, but they live longer.

In this way, two types of mating behaviour can be maintained in the same species. If more males sing, the number of flies increases. If less males sing, there will not be enough singing males for the non-singers to rely on and so more non-singing males will fail to breed. Either way, the balance between the two types of behaviour is maintained.

Because of its small size, the fly can find the singing crickets wherever they hide, but normally few other animals have the same success. Domestic cats quickly learn to hunt the crickets when there is a plague of them and the safest calling holes are all taken, forcing some males to call in the open. In Florida, a different though closely related

Calling crickets attract the attentions of a small, parasitic tachinid fly (Euphasiopteryx ochracea) that sprays the males with its larvae. The growing larvae feed on the body of the cricket and kill it.

species of cricket (*Gryllus supplicans*) is troubled by an altogether different predator, the gecko *Hemidactylus tursicus*. The gecko can locate the sound of calling male crickets, but it cannot catch them if they are protected in a burrow. Undeterred, the gecko waits patiently, and simply gobbles up the females as they arrive to mate.

Perhaps this sort of predation is what leads animals to change their signalling medium. Some species of cricket have lost their ability to sing and have only the remnants of the sound-generating rasp-and-file mechanism on their wings. They have become day-active with large, well-developed eyes. Yet others still rely on their sense of smell to find their mates and probably never used sound as a signalling system at all.

At sea, sound is tremendously important for finding mates. The sea-legends of sirens and ghost ships probably have their origins in the noises made by the humpback whale, whose eerie singing can travel many miles. On a still, fogbound morning it must have tortured the imagination of sailors, who have since taken their revenge on the whales, guided by this strange, other-wordly song.

Although humpbacks are not the only whales to sing, they are the noisiest. In winter, when both sexes come into season, they gather in shallow water in the tropics and here the males sing their lone arias. Songs are actually very complex, covering a considerable range of frequencies. A single song continues for up to twenty-five minutes and is then repeated exactly, although over a period of time the songs of individuals will change slightly. The meaning of the song pattern and the importance of the changes in it are a complete mystery, but it is likely that the songs are sung by males in order to attract females. For one thing, humpbacks do not sing at their summer feeding grounds, but only during the breeding season. Nor do males sing once they have joined a female. As yet no one has ever seen humpback whales

mating and so no one knows if this is really the final outcome of the male's long and lonely performance.

If the song of the humpback whale really is a mating call, there could hardly be a more dramatic example of the dangers inherent in advertising for a mate. Whalers have long used the songs to find their prey and have almost annihilated the humpback. Once the population numbered hundreds of thousands, but now only about 6,000 remain. Even though the humpback is protected, heavy fishing in its feeding grounds is making its recovery a painfully slow process. Sound, like sight, has its dangers, especially when it incidentally attracts that most ruthless of all predators, man.

ABOVE A humpback whale calf breaches the surface of the Atlantic. The long and lonely song of the male humpback attracts females, and the predator that almost hunted it to extinction – man.

Scent

Scent is almost a hidden world to us humans. True, we do have a sense of smell, but dog or cat owners who watch their pets carefully will quickly realize how much we are missing. It is not that our sense of smell is not powerful enough to share in the sniffing world of the dog, but that dogs can smell things that we cannot. This is what makes smell such a good medium for attracting mates. Sound and light are continuous spectra of energy, which most animals can detect; mates and predators alike. But smells are different. They are not just different wavelengths on a spectrum of energy. Each type of smell has a different character, is caused by different chemicals, and for each, animals need specific sensors.

As well as being selective, smell can be a very sensitive means of communicating. Female vapourer-moths are wingless, and when they emerge from their cocoons they rely entirely on their smell to attract their mates. Males have very well-developed antennae which can detect minute quantities of a female's scent drifting on the breeze and they can smell her up to five miles away. In fact so sensitive are the antennae that for some time biologists found it hard to believe that scent was involved at all, and some suspected that the female might be broadcasting radio waves instead, using the scent only as an aid at close range. The males' antennae certainly would not look out of place on a TV set, but now that the chemicals involved have been studied in detail most people accept that the moths' communication system is just remarkably sensitive, very specific and very effective. The scents produced by female moths have been honoured with the name of pheromones; hormones which are carried, in this case on the wind.

The vapourer-moth appears to break the fundamental rule that it is the male who takes the risks while finding a mate. In fact in most moths it is the female that attracts attention with a pheromone. In this case the moth doing the signalling is in the safest place. The female is unobtrusive, her grey-brown body difficult to spot among the cracks of the bark. Her particular scent cannot be detected by anything but a male moth, and so by advertising she does not run risks at all. Flying

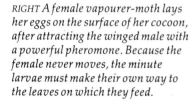

RIGHT A female vapourer-moth lays her eggs on the surface of her cocoon, after attracting the winged male with a powerful pheromone. Because the female never moves, the minute larvae must make their own way to the leaves on which they feed.

Many snakes find their mates by tasting the air for their scent. Flicking out his tongue this male grass snake collects a sample of the smells around him, then pushes its tips into a special organ on the roof of his mouth where they are analysed.

through the air in their search for a female, her potential mates are in far more danger from sharp-eyed birds than she is.

However, the southern pine bark beetle (*Dendroctonis frontalis*) shows that while pheromones may be safe, they are not infallible. The female bark beetles lay their eggs in tunnels beneath the bark, and once they have found a suitable egg-laying site, they use a pheromone which attracts both males and females so that the tree is soon the subject of a mass attack. Perhaps it is fortunate for the pine forests of the southern United States that the predatory clerid beetle (*Thanasimus dubius*) is also able to detect this pheromone and uses it to find the pine beetles. Both the adult clerid and its larvae are predators, and although they only kill two or three pine beetles a day, they may be important in controlling the spread of these pests.

The use of scent to attract males is not restricted to insects – far from it. Some fishes use pheromones to find each other, although of course here the scent is carried through the water and not through the air. During the breeding season of the channel catfish, fishermen on the Mississippi can catch enormous numbers of male catfish (*Ictalurus punctatus*) just by baiting traps with live females. The males are lured to their deaths by the pheromone which the female releases.

In the sea too, animals may use pheromones to attract mates. The larvae of the marine fish-louse *Paragnathia formica* live by sucking the blood of fishes, but before moulting to become shrimp-like adults, the male larvae burrow into mudbanks where they settle down to spend the rest of their lives. Puffs of silt from the mouth of the burrow show that it is occupied by a male, disturbing the mud as he wafts his pheromone into the water. The females he attracts are grabbed with his vice-like jaws and hauled into the burrow. Often a single male will hold a harem of up to twenty females and will fertilize each in turn as she moults. For the male paragnathia, the more effective his pheromone, the more females he will attract to his burrow and the more young he will produce.

Different again is the way in which snakes use pheromones to find each other. Female adders, and very probably many other female snakes, produce skin secretions while they are sexually receptive which they leave behind as scent trails. A male can 'taste' these by transferring the scent from his flicking tongue to two delicate sense organs in the roof of his mouth, a way of taste-smelling that has no familiar parallel in the human world. A male adder, crossing the path of a sexually receptive female, will stop and slowly turning his head from side to side and flicking his tongue in and out, he will taste the air. Remarkably, he can tell in which direction the female was travelling and will set off in pursuit, keeping himself on the trail by constantly checking the scent.

Provided that the scent cannot be detected by predators, one enormous advantage of chemical signals is that they persist after their author has disappeared. Scent marks and trails can give information to one sex about the presence of the other, even when the animal that first left the scent has moved away, something quite impossible if sight and sound are the means of communication.

The habit of leaving suitably attractive smells lying around is best developed in mammals, although these animals with their complex patterns of social behaviour make it difficult for observers to decide exactly what the smell is signalling. It may simply be informing one sex that the other is in the area, but more often than not the scents of mammals seem to carry a bewildering mixture of information about the creature's sex, breeding status, and even its position in the social hierarchy and how bad tempered it happens to be that day. Male mice, for example, are attracted to the smell of the urine of females, but avoid the smell of other males, especially males that were frightened as they urinated.

Bitches urinate more frequently when they are in heat and the smell of the urine indicates their receptivity to males. But the problem with the use of scent-marking to attract males is that finding the smell is only half the battle, since the searching animal then needs to find the individual that left the scent. Some animals leave a scent trail for prospective mates to follow. Black rhinoceroses kick through their dung piles collecting the powerful stench of their feces on their feet and leaving behind them a trail that can be followed by other animals several hours later. The black rhino has poor eyesight and leaving a scent trail is an important way of keeping in touch in this largely solitary species.

In animals with better vision, the scent-marking display itself is often visually distinctive, which allows other animals to see who is making the smell that tantalizes their nostrils. During the rut, the Bactrian camel announces his presence by urinating on his tail and then splashing the urine across his rear hump, spreading it over a wide surface area so that it evaporates quickly. If a female finds his perfume attractive, she can identify the signalling male by his rhythmic tail waving and his exaggerated legs-apart stance. The sound of his tail slapping on his rump may also help his display, advertising his presence to females upwind who cannot smell him. By combining the three modes of signalling, sight, smell and sound, he leaves little to chance.

BELOW Adult male cheetahs defend large territories, which they mark regularly with feces, scratch marks, or, as in this case, by spraying urine against a prominent land-mark.

The Third Party

When the time comes to look for a sexual partner, flowering plants face a substantially different set of problems from those encountered by animals. Plants of course cannot pull up their roots and go looking for a mate, and so for most, finding a mate first means finding an intermediary that will carry the pollen from the male part of one plant to the female part of another, and advertising for a mate means attracting the butterflies, bees, beetles, bats or birds that will do the work.

To advertise for a mate, most flowers use a combination of scent and colour, and find their go-betweens in much the same way as their animal pollinators find each other. Colour is provided by the pigmented petals, sometimes supplemented by, but more often contrasting sharply with, the surrounding leaves and bracts. Some flowers are quite dull and inconspicuous to our eyes, but they may be reflecting ultraviolet light, making them stand out like beacons to the insect pollinators at which their signals are aimed. Differences in sensitivity to the spectrum of colour help the flowers to attract specific animals, blues and yellows gripping the attention of bees, while reds attract butterflies and birds.

Yellows are particularly attractive to bees, and this snapdragon flower improves the chances that its pollen will be carried to another snapdragon by excluding most other insect species with its tightly closed lips. Only bees can open the flower, and so they tend to concentrate on this otherwise untapped nectar supply.

A Cape sugar bird perches on the flowers of a gold-tree (Leucospermum reflexum).

Flowers run a coordinated advertising campaign, and while the petals are clear visual signposts, the plant also broadcasts scents that act as additional and more specific attractants. By recognizing the smells of specific flowers, their pollinators can concentrate on a few species that are particularly rewarding. By advertising themselves to specific go-betweens, plants avoid their pollen being wasted on unrelated species which it will not be able to fertilize. As we shall see in chapter four, many plants have even more subtle ways of insisting that only a few animals act as their intermediaries.

For animals, the process of finding a mate is cooperative and in the interests of both partners. As pollinators, the go-betweens are disinterested third parties, and if they are to be employed by plants they must be rewarded for their efforts and encouraged to return. Pollen itself is a rich source of food, loaded with protein, starch, sugars and fats; the petals are advertising the ideal breakfast, at least for some hungry insects. Even among the modern descendants of the ancient cycads, pollen-eating beetles visit male cones to feed, and may accidentally transfer some pollen to female cones. Beetles were already many and varied at the time flowering plants appeared, and their chewing mouths are well suited to crunching up pollen, so it is a reasonable guess that beetles blundering around in primitive flowers were among the first intermediaries for flowering plants. Plants with simple open flowers are particularly attractive to beetles, since with their compact bodies and heavy armour they are incapable of dealing with anything too subtle. The large, accessible flowers of magnolia, the Victoria water lily and nutmeg are pollinated in this way, and all attract their go-betweens by filling the night with their scent.

Pollen may have been the original incentive which encouraged

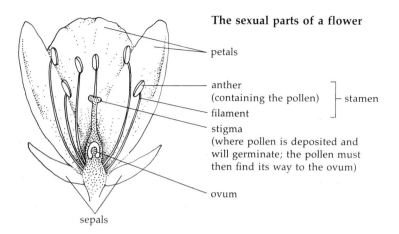

The sexual parts of a flower

petals

anther
(containing the pollen)
filament

⎤ stamen
⎦

stigma
(where pollen is deposited and
will germinate; the pollen must
then find its way to the ovum)

ovum

sepals

The magnolia flower has a simple, open structure, and the thick white anthers are sturdy enough to support clumsy insects, even those like this bug that do not normally visit flowers.

insects to skip from flower to flower, and unknowingly fertilize their hosts, but the better the beetles became at eating the pollen, the worse they became as go-betweens. Plants which use pollen as their main attractant must produce a lot of it if they are to ensure that some at least will survive to fertilize an ovule. Some flowers provide a special 'feeding pollen' easily accessible to visitors while the 'proper pollen' is almost hidden, but dusts the feeding visitor from above or behind.

Another way to protect the pollen is to produce nectar. Nectar is a rich sugary liquid which attracts insects that are not interested in the tough, crunchy pollen. By providing nectar, a plant can attract butterflies, moths, bats and humming-birds, none of which will bother with its precious pollen. Once the pollen is no longer a plant's main reward to its visitors, the pollen sacs can be tucked away where they are less easily accessible to clumsy (and greedy) beetles. The nectar can also be hidden where only the intended pollinators can reach it, its location often revealed by radiating lines of contrasting colour on the petals, that guide insects with a universal sign language. Of course, hiding the pollen and nectar cannot completely prevent undesirable visitors from finding them. Short-tongued bumble-bees have learned to bite through the backs of runner bean flowers, in order to get at the sugary liquid which they cannot reach legitimately. As a rule, however, concealing the rewards limits the range of animals that can reach them, and so improves the efficiency with which the pollen is transferred from flower to flower.

Some flowers use their attractants to ensure fidelity; others have different tricks for making sure that, at most, only a few insects can gain access to their rewards. A bee feeding on snapdragon flowers must be strong enough to crawl inside and collect the nectar. Once it has served its apprenticeship and learned how the flower works, it will continue to reap the benefits for as long as they last, obligingly responding to the flowers' special demands by becoming a specialist itself. The petals of the fly honeysuckle form a short tube, and the nectaries that lie concealed within it are easily reached by long-tongued bumble-bees. But the nectar of its close relative, the perfoliate honeysuckle, can only be reached by even longer tongues, and the plant is pollinated not by bees, but by hawk moths. In this way, some species of bees, butterflies and moths are forced to become specialists feeding on particular types of flower, to the mutual benefit of both insect and plant. The flowers save their pollen and reduce the risk of producing infertile hybrids, and the insects can specialize on particular types of flower and so avoid competing with each other for food.

chapter four

Improving the Odds

Crossing the Atlantic by sea is probably the only way to comprehend the vastness of even that relatively small ocean. In a modern liner, the journey can still take five days or more, yet almost the whole 14 million square kilometres (5½ million square miles) is the foraging ground for birds like the sooty shearwater that range from the Antarctic to Iceland and from the Gulf of Mexico to the African coast. In the Southern Hemisphere, the wandering albatross roams over an area of sea seven times the size of the Atlantic. Scattered over such a wide area, such animals cannot afford to rely on sight, sound and smell alone in order to find their mates. To breed, such creatures must improve their chances of meeting.

Breeding Seasons

One evening in the last quarter of the November moon, the Fijians take their outrigged canoes to the edge of the coral reef which surrounds their island. There they wait until midnight for the start of one of the most incredible orgies in the natural world. The start of the performance is signalled by phosphorescent trails in the water as fish begin to dart back and forth, disturbing the plankton in their wake. Soon the sea is alive with worms, millions of wriggling lengths of spaghetti, and the islanders begin scooping these out with their baskets and loading them into their canoes. By dawn the canoes are fully laden, fish lie about on the surface bloated to stupidity, and the worms have disappeared.

The swarming worms are actually only the sexual segments of a rather larger marine bristleworm, the palolo worm (*Eunice siciliensis*). The main body of the worm remains in its burrow in the coral, and only the tail section, 20 or 25 centimetres (8 or 10 inches) long, is released. This rises wriggling to the surface, and shortly after dawn it breaks up, releasing a mass of eggs and sperm into the top few inches of the sea.

With so many sperm concentrated in such a small volume, most of the eggs are quickly fertilized, even though they do not release an attractant. But to achieve these concentrations in the open sea, the release of gametes must be very closely synchronized. In the case of

OPPOSITE *The moon jellyfish (Aurelia aurita) releases its gametes at sunset. Such synchrony improves the chances that eggs and sperm will eventually meet.*

BELOW *The palolo worm is considered a gift from the gods, not to be sold but given away to friends and relatives. When the worms rise in deep water, villagers go out to collect them in canoes, scooping them from the surface in baskets of coconut fronds lined with mosquito netting. On the more prosperous island of Vanua Levu, Fiji, the worms rise over a shallow reef and are scooped up with plastic sieves and loaded into pots.*

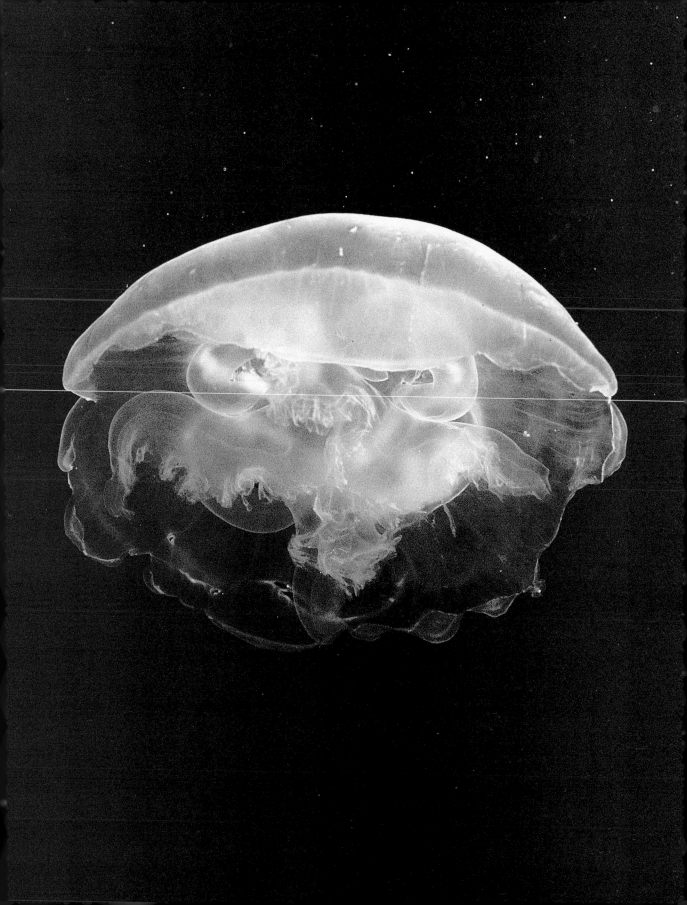

OPPOSITE A sponge releases a cloud of sperm. Sponges have several ways of ensuring that their eggs and sperm mature together. Some are sexually mature only at certain seasons, others only at certain phases of the moon.

the palolo worm it is so precisely and predictably synchronized with the November moon that the islanders can use the swarming to mark the start of the Fijian New Year, a time for feasting on slabs of the boiled worm which are sent like wedding cake across the country. A few worms may appear on the day before the rising and a few on the day after, but for the rest of the year they remain safely in their burrows.

Although the spectacular precision of the palolo worms' annual performance is unusual, breeding in synchrony with the phases of the moon is actually quite common. The Mediterranean sea urchin, *Centrochinus setons*, spawns at each full moon during the summer. The edible oyster has a two-week cycle, spawning at the full moon and again when the moon is new. The brown alga *Dictyota dichotoma* (the common forked-tongue seaweed) releases its gametes in phase with the half-moon, concentrating them further by restricting the release to a brief fifteen-minute period shortly before dawn.

Many animals ensure precise breeding synchrony by releasing their eggs and sperm as soon as they detect gametes from the opposite sex in the water; once one starts, they all start. Spawning in the oviparous oyster (*Gryphaea virginica*) is triggered by the presence of gametes in water that passes over the animals' gills. The sperm carry a hormone which causes rhythmic contractions in the muscle of the female so that

BELOW When other plant life is dying the ivy bursts into flower, attracting a large number of pollinators.

after a few minutes the eggs are forced out in a fan-shaped cloud. In a similar way, eggs stimulate the release of sperm from male oysters. The system is much the same in corals, and it is also widespread in sea urchins, starfishes and marine worms. Effective though the method may be for precise synchronization, all these animals must follow external cues, such as the sun, the moon, the temperature or the tides, so that when the signal is given, the stored eggs and sperm are mature and ready to be released.

Similar breeding synchrony is familiar enough on land, although here it is more often influenced by the sun than by the moon. Many plants have specific breeding seasons, bluebells flowering in spring while ivy ensures a superabundance of pollinators by flowering in autumn. Moreover many flowers open only at certain times of the day, a fact well known to country people who gave them names like 'Jack go to bed at noon', 'night-flowering campion' and 'four o'clock plant'. Cultivated plants selected for this behaviour formed the basis for elaborate flowering clocks that were once popular in city parks.

Like plants, land animals often concentrate their breeding efforts into a fairly brief spell, organizing things so that the young will be born when food is plentiful. Blue tits are frequent visitors to winter bird tables where they specialize in taking nuts or fat hung out of reach of larger and clumsier birds. But the young blue tits that hatch in late April or May have to be fed on a high protein diet of caterpillars, that themselves feed on the succulent new growth of spring.

The caterpillar season itself is brief. They hatch from their eggs as the buds begin to break, and must be fully grown before the leaves of their woodland food trees have become tough and loaded with the protective chemicals which make mature leaves difficult to digest. The blue tits must time their nestbuilding and egg-laying with uncanny accuracy, and they do this by being sensitive to changes in the length of the day. As the days grow longer in spring, the sexual organs of the male and female begin to develop and manufacture the sperm and eggs that will start the new generation. This sensitivity of birds to day length has been cleverly exploited by poultry farmers who keep their birds laying throughout the year by creating an artificial spring day-length, which every back-yard poultry keeper knows is the time when normal hens lay the most eggs.

In equatorial regions, the subtle changes in daylength are an un-reliable signal for breeding, and animals must find other ways to anticipate the breeding season. The sight of green grass is one stimu-lus that causes young African red-billed quelea to moult into breeding plumage and begin nestbuilding, although older birds may learn other more subtle signs and begin breeding earlier. Even in temperate regions, animals often ignore the solar calendar when their success depends on other factors. Spadefoot toads, for example, begin breed-ing immediately after heavy rain, which falls in midsummer in Mexico, but in spring or autumn in California. Spawning in fishes may be triggered by temperature changes rather than changes in the day length, a rising temperature stimulating spring-spawning fishes,

In the Seychelles, fairy terns ignore the seasons and breed every ten months.

while autumn-spawning species become sexually active as the water begins to cool. Where the food supply is constant, animals will often forgo the benefits of breeding in synchrony and adopt their own rhythm, raising young at whatever interval suits their physiology.

This carefree lifestyle is in sharp contrast to life in temperate climes. The summer with its sometimes brief flush of growth is followed by the hard and hungry days of winter, forcing most animals to observe precisely timed breeding seasons. For the roe deer, the demands are so severe that mating and breeding have been separated. The rut occurs in autumn when all the animals are well fed, but not until December does the fertilized egg become implanted in the uterus. Badgers ovulate immediately after giving birth, but if the egg is fertilized, its implantation will be delayed for up to nine months. During this period the female has the advantage of carrying a fertile embryo but does not suffer the strain of supporting its growth until conditions improve in the following spring.

Synchronizing reproductive behaviour makes it more likely that eggs and sperm will eventually meet. However, accurate synchrony is most important for those that leave the task of finding each other to the gametes themselves. Partners that pair before spawning can be more independent. True, the partners must release their gametes at the same moment, but to a large extent they can ignore the rest of the population, making the virtuosity displayed by the palolo worm unnecessary. More sophisticated animals whose eggs are fertilized internally have even more flexibility, since the female can store the sperm until her eggs are ripe. But even animals whose eggs are fertilized internally often breed only at certain seasons. By concentrating their mate-finding exertions into a short breeding season, males and females can coordinate their search and improve their chances of finding each other. Also, by arranging things so that the young are born at a time of plenty, the parents increase their chances of breeding successfully.

Habitat

A nightingale sings from the depths of a hazel thicket.
Nightingales breed in scrub with a dense undergrowth,
and hazel coppice with its thick shrub layer provides
ideal habitat. On returning to Europe from their
wintering grounds in tropical Africa, the nightingales
search out suitable nesting areas where their
magnificent song can be heard at dusk and dawn
throughout the spring. Female nightingales first settle in
a suitable patch of habitat where they feed and recover
their strength after their migration, and presumably
move elsewhere if they do not hear a suitable mate. By
looking for a mate in the most likely place, the birds
considerably improve their chances of finding each
other. The same is true for many, many other animals of
course, but this method for improving the chances of
finding a mate is so obvious that it is easily overlooked.
The nightingale that sang in Berkeley Square was almost
certainly wasting his time – few females would visit
such an unpromising nesting site.

'Marriage'

The purpose of marriage, at least according to *The Book of Common Prayer,* is the avoidance of sin, a timely reminder of the dangers in using such familiar terms to describe animal behaviour. Everyday words like marriage and divorce, mean different things to different people, and consciously or subconsciously it is easy to let our moral judgments distort our understanding when we use words like these to describe what is going on in the natural world. Birds like the wren can find themselves labelled as squalidly promiscuous little beasts, while swans, which mate for life, become virtue incarnate. To put it another way, what we think we see may not be what we are looking at.

Biologists usually avoid the term marriage altogether, and use serious-sounding phrases like 'lifetime mate fidelity', only to fall back on 'divorce' instead of the even-more cumbersome 'separation of partners in which fidelity might otherwise have been expected'.
It is easy to see why.

'Marriage' between animals has very little to do with the avoidance of sin, but a great deal to do with ensuring that as many offspring as possible survive. Very few animals mate for life, indeed few enough even restrict themselves to one sexual partner at a time. While there may be many reasons for fidelity, one important consequence is that those animals which get 'married' need not waste time searching for a mate in the future.

Tradition

The purple emperor butterfly is a large and very beautiful inhabitant of the oak woods of western Europe through temperate Asia to Japan. Its iridescent purple wings make it a favourite target of collectors, and throughout much of its range it is threatened with local extinction. The adults are rarely seen on the woodland floor, but occasionally they descend from the treetops to drink from puddles or to feed on animal dung, which they do with relish. But this is not the strangest of their habits, for the purple emperor has a very unusual life history.

Purple emperor caterpillars feed almost exclusively on one plant, the broad-leaved sallow, *Salix caprea*. The food plants must face north, protected from direct summer sunlight which can kill the larvae. The adult female butterflies lay only a few eggs on each suitable plant before moving on to the next, so not surprisingly the larvae are scattered far and wide through the wood. While other butterflies faced with similar problems use pheromones to attract mates, or search the woods for a distinctive flash of colour, the purple emperor adults congregate at a particular tree, the Master Oak, where they court and mate. What is special about this tree, no one knowns. Usually it is set a

OPPOSITE ABOVE On the Greek island of Rhodes, thousands of moths (Panaxia quadripunctata) gather in a single valley where they rest throughout the summer before mating and dispersing to lay their eggs.

OPPOSITE BELOW LEFT The spectacular migrations of salmon concentrate the fish into a relatively small area where finding a mate is comparatively straightforward.

BELOW A male purple emperor butterfly perches on the master oak. All the purple emperors in a locality will gather at this traditional meeting place to court.

little apart, perhaps on a slight rise, but often it seems to be just another tree in the wood, at least to human eyes. The purple emperor's eyes are more discerning. The butterflies identify the master oak, year after year, and if it is cut down, the colony may suffer severely.

How the purple emperor identifies its courtship tree is a complete mystery. The larvae have had no opportunity to learn the site from their parents, yet it seems inconceivable that they should be genetically programmed to seek out a particular tree and recognize it by features that we cannot distinguish. Fortunately not all animals which use traditional mating sites are quite so puzzling.

The migrations of salmon and turtles to their breeding grounds are phenomenal feats of navigation, but unlike the purple emperor, these creatures have the scent of their home river (or for the turtles their home beach) fixed firmly in their memories. Both these very different animals find their breeding grounds largely through using their sense of smell. A salmon can recognize the waters of its home river from well out at sea, and green turtles pick up the smell of Ascension Island from the coast of Brazil, almost 1,900 kilometres (1,200 miles) away. Eels may use a combination of smell, ocean currents, and their remarkable ability to steer by the stars in their even longer journey from the rivers of Europe to their breeding grounds in the Sargasso Sea, a staggering 5,600 kilometres (3,500 miles).

These spectacular migrations result in massive concentrations of animals. Pacific salmon once swam almost shoulder to shoulder in the headstreams of rivers like the Sacramento and San Joaquin in California. In the sea, off the coast of Costa Rica, thousands of leatherback turtles assemble to mate and lay their eggs along a single 35-kilometre (22-mile) stretch of beach. Once they have found their home, finding a

mate is hardly a problem. (In fact for female turtles avoiding mates may be the main preoccupation, since mating is a violent and sometimes wounding business.) It would, however, be a mistake to think that these migrations serve only to collect the animals together. Adult leatherback turtles feed almost entirely on eel-grass, and the population that nests on the beach at Tortuguero spends the rest of its life feeding in the area of Miskito bank, off the coast of Nicaragua. The breeding migration certainly brings large numbers together, but it is unlikely that males and females could not find each other at their feeding grounds if they chose to do so. At Tortuguero, safety from predators, a suitable nesting beach and food for the young may be just as important as the mating aggregation.

Once the habit of breeding in a particular location has been established and a species becomes genetically programmed to return to the place of its birth for mating, the habit may be hard to break. When the ancestors of the common eel first began making their journey from the rivers of Europe to the sea, it is unlikely that they travelled 3,000 miles to reach their goal. Changing climate, ocean currents and even the

The green turtle lays its soft, leathery eggs on a secluded beach in the Heron Islands. As with many animals that aggregate in large numbers, the suitability and safety of the nest site can be more important than the relative ease with which the animals can now find mates.

A 'club' of young gannets. These are probably all birds that were not ready to breed when the season began, because they were unfit or immature. Although they do not breed, club birds rehearse the full range of breeding behaviour, protecting 'nest' sites and courting with 'mates'. In some other birds, this sort of behaviour establishes a pair that will remain together for life, but not in gannets. A male must defend a suitable nest site at the start of the season before he can attract a female.

spreading of the Atlantic floor may have combined to turn what began as a jaunt to the sea into an epic journey which the eels are now forced to repeat. To adopt an alternative breeding system would require too many coincidental changes, and the present system is quite adequate until a creature evolves which is as efficient at exploiting the eels' freshwater home but capable of breeding without such an exhausting mating migration.

Birds that return to traditional nesting sites to mate are not so tied by the bonds of tradition and it is not unusual for a bird to change colonies during its life. Nonetheless, the tendency of seabirds to return and breed on the rock on which they were born is at least partly responsible for some of the most impressive sights in the natural world: three rocky stacks around St Kilda are the nesting site for 100,000 gannets; an estimated two million breeding pairs of great shearwater pack themselves onto Nightingale Island in Tristan da Cunha; an incredible ten million Chinstrap penguins breed on the tiny island of Zavoderski at the edge of the Antarctic pack ice.

By aggregating into large groups, birds reduce the problems of finding a mate quite considerably, and the habit is best developed in seabirds, almost all of which nest in dense colonies. Often these are packed tightly onto a single rock or a short stretch of coastline, a traditional site where the same birds breed year after year.

These colonies are more than mere meeting-places. They are always sited within foraging distance of a reliable food source which will sustain the enormous number of birds through the breeding season. To untrained human eyes the oceans look like a uniform desert, but around the world wherever deep ocean currents well up bringing nutritious minerals to the sunlit surface, a bloom of plankton feeds a chain of small invertebrates, fishes, and their predators. These up-welling currents are responsible for the massive concentrations of Antarctic krill which provide food for many animals, including by far the commonest of Antarctic birds, the penguins.

Colonial living makes finding mates a relatively simple task, but this is not its main purpose for birds like the chinstrap penguin. The colony sits, almost literally, on top of a considerable food supply, and the birds have no need to move far from their nest during the breeding season. The colony has become important to the penguins' breeding in another way. The social contact with other pairs close by stimulates the birds, causing their ovaries and testes to develop faster than they would in isolated individuals. This stimulation is important in synchronizing the breeding of the colony and also in stimulating the birds to lay early since, as in kittiwakes, the first young to fledge are the most likely to survive.

This may explain why some birds pack their nests into a ridiculously small area and ignore other sites which seem equally well suited to breeding. Sometimes there may be subtle differences between superficially similar nest sites, differences in the slope or shape of nesting ledges, or in the protection which an outcrop can provide from predators. The guillemot prefers to nest on long ledges, where many birds can fit together side by side and the availability of suitable nest sites may limit the size of the colony. But it is unusual for birds to be quite so choosey. More often than not, no such differences can be found between the site and the neighbouring islands. As with the great shearwaters of Tristan da Cunha, the birds simply choose to congregate in their two-million strong colony. Great shearwaters normally nest in burrows, but in some years the colony is so densely packed that some of the birds are forced to nest on the surface, because all possible burrowing sites on the island have been taken. Yet nearby are dozens of small islands, geologically and ecologically almost identical. While it is hard to believe that social stimulation requires as many as two million other birds, it is obvious that no one wants to be the first to go off and start a new colony.

Because birds which nest in colonies are reluctant to pioneer new breeding sites, it can be very difficult to re-establish colonies that have been destroyed. In an attempt to re-introduce puffins to an island off the east coast of Canada, the illusion of a thriving colony was created by planting dummy birds on the cliff-top. The experiment proved successful, and the same trick is now being tried in other countries, and with other species of bird.

Penguins come together in their millions to exploit an abundant supply of food, and other seabirds like the guillemot may be forced into the colonial habit by a shortage of nesting sites. For the ocean wanderers like the albatross and the shearwaters, neither explanation seems to be quite sufficient; most species breed at a considerable distance from their feeding grounds. Birds may have to forage up to a thousand miles from the nest, leaving their mates to keep the egg warm in sub-zero temperatures for over a week. Once the egg has hatched, the returning bird regurgitates its load of fish oil for the young chick, while its partner, the fast almost over, flies off in search of a well-earned meal. The Laysan albatross will lose up to a quarter of its weight during each stint of incubation.

With such distances to travel between their feeding grounds and their colony, food supply is hardly likely to be the cause of such dense nesting. Nor apparently is the availability of nest sites limited. Yet year after year the birds return, usually to exactly the same spot, guided by the sun, the stars, their sense of magnetism and finally their memory of the site from previous years. Here an established pair can once again renew their association. If last year's mate fails to reappear there are plenty of others, bereaved birds as well as first-time nesters, all looking for mates. In some species, most of the world's population

Mating garter snakes. The large female, who has just emerged from hibernation, is at the centre of the bundle.

will be gathered in the same place and a lost mate can usually be replaced in time to breed that same year.

Although the colonial habit may help wandering seabirds find their mates, this is probably not the whole story. The sooty albatross, at sea the most solitary of the family, is also a solitary nester. If the function of albatross colonies were primarily to help birds locate potential mates, then this is the exact opposite of what we would expect. Solitary birds may have to search for days in order to find a mate, losing valuable breeding time. While for some species the colonial habit provides protection from predators, gives social stimulation and improves the chances that bereaved and inexperienced birds will find mates, there must also be disadvantages which force birds like the sooty albatross to adopt a more solitary habit, but why they do this remains a mystery.

Birds are not alone in using traditional meeting places to help them make a rapid start to the breeding season. There is an unexpected parallel between the behaviour of colonial seabirds and the habits of the red-sided garter snake, the most northerly reptile in North America. In autumn, these harmless snakes collect in enormous numbers at traditional hibernating dens, where they spend the winter in a state of complete torpor. As the sun begins to warm the ground in spring, the snakes emerge in their thousands. Males follow females as they leave, and cluster round them, each one trying to work himself into a position in which he can copulate. In the writhing mating balls, up to a hundred males can cluster around each female, although less than thirty are usually involved. At the peak of the mating season the dens are strewn with mating balls, heaving and twisting, changing shape and size as the males join or leave a group. So powerful is the stimulation of the female's pheromone that males will chase females up into bushes and trees and even attempt to copulate with dead females. Once mated, a female loses her attractive smell and moves off into the undergrowth unmolested, while the males stay behind to try their luck again.

Like the colonial nesting of seabirds, the communal hibernation of garter snakes helps the animals to begin breeding at the first possible moment in spring. For garter snakes, as for most seabirds, finding a mate is made easier by the way in which the animals congregate at certain seasons, but this may be almost coincidental to the main purpose of the aggregation. As for animals which live in social groups throughout their lives, being part of a group has many advantages quite apart from making it easy to find a mate. There are more eyes to watch for predators, and more beaks to peck at them. Even if the cooperative defence system fails, there is less chance of being the victim. Animals that live in groups can learn from each other, co-operate to hunt for prey, and look after each other's infants, all of which helps to raise the young to maturity. As we shall see in the next section, however, animals that live permanently in social groups must often go outside the group to mate, in order to avoid the unfortunate consequences of inbreeding.

Becoming More Specialized

All plants that attract pollinators improve the chances that their pollen will reach the right stigma by offering rewards that are only to the taste of certain go-betweens. Even so, bees, moths and butterflies may be laden with pollen from half a dozen or more species of plants.

In an attempt to find an intermediary not already involved in another relationship, plants often attract unusual pollinators. Hummingbirds, sunbirds and honey creepers have all evolved in response to the plants' search for more faithful pollinators, but they need to consume more calories than cold-blooded insects just to stay alive, and so the flowers must pay for these specialist services by producing more nectar. Bats are more economical pollinators, at least in semi-temperate areas, since they hibernate through the winter and the plants do not need to keep them supplied with food the whole year round. Where there are no bats to compete with, other small mammals like the honey possum and the mouse lemur are seduced by the plants into playing the same role, feeding on nectar and collecting the pollen on their furry snouts.

To obtain extreme fidelity, plants often resort to deceit, and the

The Madagascan orchid (Angraecum sesquipedale) has found an unusual way of obtaining an exclusive relationship with its pollinator. The large, white petals taper into a foot-long spur. Inside, and right at the bottom of this narrow gullet, lie the plant's nectaries, apparently completely inaccessible. When this flower was first discovered, no one dared guess at how it might be pollinated until it was shown to Charles Darwin. He suggested that somewhere on the island there must live an insect, perhaps a large moth, with a tongue long enough to reach to the bottom of this bizarre flower. His idea caused considerable amusement to entomologists, until the insect was discovered almost forty years later. Called Xanthopan morgani praedicta, the last part of the name is a sort of apology to the great man.

OPPOSITE Fly orchid (Ophrys insectifera).

RIGHT The wasp (Argogorytes mystaceus) attempting to copulate with a fly orchid (Ophrys insectifera). The male's copulatory apparatus is partly erected at the tip of his abdomen, and his thrusts have exposed the pollen sacs near his head.

BELOW Hidden among a tangle of branches, the flowers of Protea humiflora are inaccessible to most animals and birds, and open only at night. They are pollinated by small rodents like the Namaqua rock mouse, which uses the branches as a platform when sipping nectar from the flower. During its visit, the mouse's nose gets dusted with pollen, which it carries to the next flower.

colourful displays and powerful smells with which they appeal to pollinators are not always legitimate advertisements. Some, like the arum lilies, advertise goods that are definitely not in stock, imitating the smell of dung, carrion or animal skin, the last of these being the scent of *Arum conophalloides* which attracts hairy blood-sucking midges. These become trapped in the base of the leaf-like bract which surrounds the flower, where they crawl around for a day and a night, wandering over the female flowers (and depositing any pollen they are carrying). As the flower ages, the hairs that held the flies prisoner begin to wither and they crawl to freedom across the male parts of the flower, becoming completely covered with pollen as they go. The scent of the arum is so convincing to the flies that they soon fall for the same ruse again, this time transferring the pollen they have collected to the female flowers of the next plant.

Many orchids are even more selective, broadcasting their advertisements on a wavelength to which very few creatures are sensitive. The fly orchid, *Ophrys insectifera* makes quite certain that little of its pollen goes to waste. Instead of restricting itself to a few insects that are roughly the right shape and size, the flower attracts only the males of a single species of wasp, *Argogorytes mystaceus*, a remarkable specificity which it achieves by imitating the pheromone released by the female. In early spring, when the wasps first emerge, the males can be found searching in the grass for the source of the scent emanating from the very first flowers. Later, a male downwind of a fly orchid will turn sharply and head straight for his goal. Once he finds the orchid he attempts to mate with the lip of the flower, which to our eyes is a none-too-cunning imitation of the female wasp. The furriness of the lip may provide the right feel, barren nectaries play the role of the female wasp's eyes, while part of the flower appears to be imitating the insect's antennae. These reassuring sights and textures are all the male needs to confirm that he has found a female and he begins to copulate. As he attempts to mate, his thrusts force the protective covers from the sticky sacs which contain the pollen, and the sacs become glued to the insect. Although the wasp gropes with his abdomen and extends his sexual apparatus, he eventually gives up and flies off to another flower, where the pollen sacs will be deposited.

A similar exclusive relationship has evolved between the yucca plant and the yucca moth. The yucca, now popular as a houseplant, originally comes from the southern United States and Mexico, where it is pollinated by a small moth called *Tegiticula yuccasella*. The adult moth does not feed at all, but nevertheless the female collects the putty-like pollen, and holding it in a small ball beneath her chin she squashes it on to a ripe stigma. At first this seems impossible, it is almost as if the moth feels sorry for the poor yucca plant, which because of the relative position of its stamens and anthers is completely incapable of pollinating itself. But no; once the pollen has been loaded on to the stigma, the female moth lays her eggs in the ovary, so that her larvae can feed on the seeds. Fortunately for the yucca plant, enough seeds survive unharmed to raise a new generation.

The dodo, whose extinction may have had unexpected consequences for the tambalacoque tree.

This sort of specialization carries with it a serious risk. While there are enough flowers to feed all the moth larvae and enough moths to fertilize all the flowers each year, the system works very nicely. But should something happen to the moths, then the plant is also doomed. The tambalacoque tree may have suffered through being over-dependent, not on its pollinator but on the animal which dispersed its seeds. It is now almost extinct on its native island of Mauritius, and recently only thirteen specimens of this large and once-common tree survived. All were over 300 years old and dying, and no seedlings at all could be found, although every year the trees produced a good crop of apparently fertile seeds, wrapped in a pulpy, succulent fruit.

It may be coincidence that the seeds stopped germinating at about the same time as the dodo became extinct. The dodo's disappearance in 1681 is probably the most infamous case of extinction for which man has been responsible, and although we actually know sadly little about the life of this pathetically comic, large and flightless bird, it might well have fed on the fruits of the tambalacoque tree. Its crushing gizzard would have been large enough to crack open the seeds before depositing them, with a heap of fertilizer, well away from their source.

This explanation of the demise of the tambalacoque tree is controversial. Many tropical forest trees germinate only sporadically and uncracked seeds have recently germinated in nursery plots. If the extinction of the dodo really was responsible for the failure of the seeds to germinate naturally, it is hard to imagine a better example of the dangers of overdependence on a single animal for such an important part of the life-cycle. In the hard-fought game of co-evolution, the tambalacoque tree seems to have reached the ultimate goal – an exclusive relationship with a single animal – until by wiping out the dodo, man moved the goalposts.

chapter five

Avoiding the Problems

The doormouse must go to considerable
trouble to find a mate, and then faces an
increased risk of being eaten while he
copulates. Blackberries, however, suffer
few of the hardships associated with sex:
they have simply given it up.

The Best of Both Worlds

Roughly half way between Europe and North America lies the mid-Atlantic ridge, a crack at the bottom of the ocean which exudes molten lava from a gaping wound in the earth's crust. Associated with it are wonderful life-forms, flourishing on chemicals from the earth's molten core. But this abundance on the ocean floor is a tiny oasis in a dark desert. Life of any sort is rare, and the few fish that have been caught in these depths are all bones and teeth. Brought bursting to the deck of a ship, most reveal one other common characteristic: they are neither male nor female but hermaphrodites, both sexes at once.

Strange beings like the lizard fish and the lancet fish find little to eat in their deep-water home. Equally important, they go for weeks on end without meeting another individual of the same species. In such circumstances it is hardly surprising that they have developed a method of reproduction that reduces the problems of sex. Being hermaphrodite doubles the chances that any meeting will be productive, for since every individual is both male and female, everyone else of that species is a suitable mate.

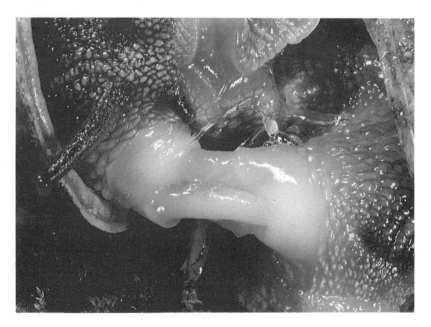

Snails ready to copulate crawl about slowly, often pausing with the front ends of their bodies lifted in the air. When two snails meet, they rear up and press their feet firmly together. Then swaying from side to side, they caress each other with their tentacles and secrete masses of slime. After several hours, each partner injects a copulatory dart into the other, which seems to hurt but nevertheless results in a renewed bout of tentacle caressing. The actual process of mating requires a lot of delicate manoeuvring, since snails are hermaphrodite and each must insert its penis into the other.

Thus, rare animals can find a mate, but being hermaphrodite must have other functions too. On land there is a wealth of hermaphrodite plants, many of which grow cheek by jowl in dense clumps. Hermaphroditism is also widespread among creatures like slugs and worms which are far from rare.

In order to understand why some animals are hermaphrodite and others not, consider the slug. Slugs, though hermaphrodites, are unable to fertilize themselves and need to find a partner. Imagine a mutant slug that has lost the ability to be female, and so is no longer a hermaphrodite but a straightforward, sexual male. Clearly this slug cannot put any energy into making slugs' eggs, so instead he concentrates all his efforts on being a male and slides around the garden fertilizing as many hermaphrodites as he can. By not making eggs, he saves energy, and if this enables him to fertilize more than twice as many females as a normal slug, the number of all-male slugs will increase each year. Once there are all-male slugs around, all-females slugs will also appear because, as we have already seen, the number of females will tend to balance the number of males. Eventually the hermaphrodites would become extinct.

In fact, for real slugs, snails and earthworms, this has not happened, and the reason is probably that the all-male mutant cannot fertilize twice as many eggs as the normal, hermaphrodite version. It is easy to see why. All these self-incompatible hermaphrodites are very, very slow. An all-male slug cannot scamper about the garden sowing wild oats everywhere he goes. Not only is he slow, but because he is a prisoner in a slug's body, he is unable to move around and mate at all if the weather is too hot or dry. Then, once he does find a mate, the process of courtship and mating itself is slow and laborious; slugs first circle around each other secreting mucus, often for several hours, before twisting together in a slimy embrace and exchanging sperm. There is no reason to suppose that mating could be any faster for our mutant male slug.

The Don Juan of the slug world faces a tough task, particularly since being hermaphrodite has advantages of its own. A hermaphrodite that cannot hope to fertilize large numbers of eggs accepts its role as both male and female. It can then save energy by producing only enough sperm to fertilize its partner's eggs. Instead of investing equal effort into male and female roles, hermaphrodites can economize on sperm and use the energy that they save to produce more eggs.

Then there is a second advantage to being both sexes at once. For many animals and plants, there comes a point in the season when the females are no longer fertile, and instead of producing gametes they concentrate their energies on looking after their young. Flowers catch the last rays of the autumn sun and provide food to nourish and 'set' their seed. Mothers feed and brood their young. Meanwhile the males can do nothing, but hermaphrodites make good use of their time. First they can play both roles and mutually fertilize each other. That done, the male role can be dispensed with, and they can begin concentrating on their female role, taking care of their eggs. For plants and slow-

Hazel catkins shedding pollen. The separate, female flower can be seen at the tip of the branch.

moving animals that cannot be taken over by specialist males, hermaphroditism really is the best of both worlds.

Plants have a further decision to make which does not trouble the animal world at all. If a plant is to be hermaphrodite, should it keep its male and female organs together, or should the male and female flowers be separate but still on the same plant? Plants that advertise for pollinators gain nothing by separating the two sexes, since they must attract their go-betweens to both male and female organs. When plants do have separate male and female flowers, they usually do not advertise at all, but instead are pollinated by the wind.

Wind pollination seems crude and haphazard when compared with the beautiful precision with which animals can be enticed to move pollen from flower to flower. While some plants, like pines and firs, have probably always been wind pollinated, wind-pollinated flowering plants almost certainly evolved from ancestors that were once insect-pollinated. By doing without insect go-betweens, wind-pollinated plants benefit in several ways. They can flower in early spring, before the insects take to the air in sufficient numbers, and they save by not producing the rewards and attractants that animal pollinators require. Many wind-pollinated plants – grasses, nettles, pines and firs – live in dense stands which flower only briefly. For these plants, wind pollination may be necessary because with so many flowers to be pollinated at once, there are not enough insects to do all the work at the right time of year.

Whatever advantages they gain, these plants all face similar problems. They must produce enormous amounts of pollen and keep it dry so that it does not stick together. Though sheltered from the rain it must be exposed to the wind. By contrast, the female must filter as large a volume of air as possible in order to trap the precious pollen. The requirements of male and female flowers are often contradictory, and many wind-pollinated plants have lost their hermaphrodite flowers and separated the two sexes. Usually the separate flowers are still kept on the same plant, but in some species, among them poplar, juniper and cannabis, the male and female flowers are on different plants, and other examples are found scattered throughout the plant kingdom. The male flowers usually hang in catkins. Their umbrella-shaped scales protect the pollen from the rain; but in dry weather the anthers are held out on long filaments, and the pollen is released to be carried on the wind. Some catkins are even more sophisticated, trapping the pollen between the scales so that it is released only when bouncing in the wind. Nettle flowers flick out their anthers as they open, releasing all their pollen in a single puff which can easily be seen by anybody who patiently watches a nettle-bed on a summer's day.

The female flowers of wind-pollinated plants are also very distinctive. Usually the stigma is large, feathery and often sticky, with each flower containing only one, or at most a few seeds, which are carefully protected. The stigma cannot hope to collect enough of the drifting pollen to fertilize more, unless, like maize, the plants grow in dense clumps where the air will quickly fill with pollen.

By returning to a primitive sexual strategy, dispensing with the services of insects and adapting to make the best use of the wind for pollination, plants like the firs and the birches have even been able to colonize the bleak Arctic tundra. Hostile environments like the tundra often make sex difficult for plants and animals and, as we shall see in the next section, many plants and even some animals have taken what are apparently even more regressive steps, becoming self-fertile hermaphrodites, or even completely asexual in order to avoid the problems that are constantly associated with sex.

Self-fertilization

The Holy Island of Lindisfarne lies close to the border between England and Scotland, separated from the Northumberland coast by saltmarshes and mudflats. At low tide, tourists pour across to explore the castle and the ancient priory, or to watch the wildfowl which gather here on migration. When the tide turns, the island is cut off and the sea deposits a layer of mud on the road, along with bits of seaweed, driftwood and the seeds of plants that thrive in the saltmarsh.

As the road reappears, these seeds are picked up on car tyres or splashed up to stick beneath mudguards as the tourists begin their journey home along the northern roads. Then, as the mud dries, the seeds drop off again and bounce across the tarmac before coming to rest in the soil at the edge of the road. Surprisingly they can germinate and grow here, for the environment is much like their saltmarsh home. Salt spread to prevent icing in winter has been washed off the roads and into the soil, providing ideal conditons for the plants. They germinate, they grow and they flower ... only to find themselves perhaps several hundred miles from the nearest source of pollen. Yet the sea aster, sea spurrey and sea orache have multiplied successfully and now decorate motorways from Holy Island well into central England. What makes this possible is that all these plants are self-fertile hermaphrodites and can pollinate themselves.

Being self-fertile is obviously very useful for plants whose survival depends on continually colonizing new ground as soon as a suitable patch appears. But it carries with it one big disadvantage. Instead of shuffling the genetic material and creating new combinations of traits which might succeed in the struggle to survive, continuous self-fertilization eventually produces a set of look-alikes. Within ten generations the plants become almost identical copies of each other, able to survive perfectly well in the conditions which suit them best, but without the variation which will help them to expand their range and occupy new territory where the demands are slightly different. Should the conditions change, the family's only chance for survival is to colonize a new site, where things are like they used to be back home. This is not a forlorn hope. Plants like the sea aster are adapted to life in an environment which changes in just this way. As one section of salt marsh rises from the sea and turns to scrub, another area of

Lindisfarne, off the coast of Northumberland, is cut off by every high tide.

marshland will probably begin to form further along the coast, and plants that did adapt as the marsh dried out would actually be at a disadvantage when the time came to move to a new site. The weeds of disturbed ground and woodland glades are further examples of plants adapted to this inevitable cycle. They too produce large numbers of seeds to ensure their transfer to new sites, and like the sea aster, many are self-fertile.

In familiar animals, things are usually the other way around. Separating the sexes is an effective way of encouraging outbreeding, and by contrast it is the hermaphrodites that seem peculiar and need special explanation. In fact hermaphrodite animals are common, but because no mammals or birds are hermaphrodite, we persist in thinking it is something strange. Earth worms, slugs, snails, flatworms and many marine animals are always hermaphrodite, as are many sponges and sea anemones, and yet as we have seen, these animals cross-fertilize each other, the male part of one giving sperm to the female part of the other.

There are many hermaphrodites, but few can fertilize themselves. Self-fertile animals, like self-fertile plants, lose the advantages of producing varied offspring, and like the self-fertile plants, they are uncommon. Animal weeds, they specialize in colonizing new territories. The killifish (*Rivulus marmoratus*) is one of the few self-

Sea aster (Aster tripolium), growing in its salt-marsh home.

fertilizing vertebrates, and it lives in coastal ponds in Florida and on islands in the Gulf of Mexico which are alternately flooded and then dried out. Presumably the killifish often finds itself alone as its pond refills, and the ability to fertilize itself makes the difference between life and death for the family line. Self-fertilization is also quite common in freshwater snails, and again it is not difficult to believe that this might be an advantage in the small and unpredictable ponds which these specialized animals inhabit.

Renouncing Sex

Most plants go to extraordinary lengths to achieve cross-fertilization. By contrast a few, like the sea aster, sacrifice the advantages of out-breeding for the chance to invade isolated habitats. Others have given up sex altogether. The cottony seeds of dandelions which float around the garden in summer are produced asexually; none is fertilized and each seed germinates and grows into a plant identical to its parents. This particular type of asexual reproduction, in which females produce eggs or seeds that develop into identical copies of themselves, is called parthenogenesis (from the Greek *parthenos* = virgin; *genesis* = generation).

Dandelions reproduce asexually, their feathery parachutes carrying seeds that have never been fertilized.

Virgin birth is not uncommon and examples can be found scattered throughout the plant and animal kingdoms. We have already seen that animals such as the water flea can reproduce in this way and yet switch to sexual reproduction in order to invade a new environment. Many species of stick insect have taken this a step further and done away with males altogether; these females always lay unfertilized eggs which hatch into more, identical females.

There are good reasons for believing that apart from the simple creatures like the amoebae and the blue-green algae, discussed in 'Crude Beginnings' (page 22), these plants and animals have quite recently lost the ability to reproduce sexually. Dandelions continue to produce some pollen, but now it serves no function and is simply a relic of their sexual past. The blackberry flower produces pollen, but the seedlings are still exact replicas of the mother plant. Yet without pollination the seeds cannot develop, for although the embryo itself is produced asexually, the tissue which surrounds it must be fertilized before it can begin the task of feeding the growing seedling.

There is also evidence that these animals which reproduce by parthenogenesis have only recently renounced sexual reproduction. Males are unknown for many species of stick insect, but others, often close relatives, must go through the normal procedure of finding mates and copulating before their eggs will hatch.

In the deserts of the south-western United States live three species of lizard, whose story gives a clear idea of how parthenogenetic races are started. The grasslands to the east of the Rio Grande shelter the little striped whiptail, a small, slender brown lizard with a white striped body and brown legs. In the scrubland to the west lives the western whiptail, which has a splotchy body with no stripes at all. In between the two lives one of the very few vertebrates capable of virgin birth, the whiptail lizard. It looks like a cross between its neighbours, with white stripes along its body but splotchy brown legs, and almost certainly that is exactly what it is – a hybrid incapable of breeding with either of its parents, but able to reproduce on its own.

Many parthenogenetic races are the result of hybridization, and bear the tell-tale signs of their origins. One strange fish, the Amazon molly from North America, began life as a hybrid between two closely related species and although it now reproduces by virgin birth, the eggs must still make contact with the sperm from one of the parent species before they will begin to develop. Although the parent species prefer to mate with their own kind, males will attempt to fertilize the hybrid female. Which is just as well for the Amazon molly, whose continued survival depends on the males' incautious promiscuity.

A plant or animal which suddenly finds itself able to reproduce asexually gains two advantages over its sexual rivals. By doing away with males it spares itself all the aggravation of finding a mate and courting, and so can put all the energy it saves into producing females. In fact, by eliminating males, a parthenogenetic female can produce twice as many females as her sexually reproducing rivals, who are wasting half their time producing males, and very soon, simply by force of numbers, the asexual variety will take over. Of course, each fresh generation is just so many carbon copies of the original parent, but in an environment which is uniform and predictable from year to year, this may even be an advantage. Sexual plants and animals will create varied offspring, many of which are less well adapted to their surroundings and doomed to fail in the battle for space and food. By turning out endless, successful replicas of themselves, the asexual versions should soon take over and drive out the sexual competition. But they do not. Instead of displacing their sexual rivals, the completely asexual plants and animals, like the self-fertile hermaphrodites, usually lead a life of near-exile either at the edge of their parents' range or on deserted islands. Not only are they exiled, but in evolutionary terms they are also doomed. No completely asexual plant or animal has ever gone on to found its own dynasty, to develop a complete branch of Nature's tree. Always they are mere twigs, a species here, perhaps a genus there. Until now we have assumed that the advantage of sex lies in its ability to combine two favourable mutations from different organisms, but is this enough to explain the maintenance of sex in the face of competition from asexual mutants that are twice as good at producing offspring as their parents? In the long run, the asexual mutants may be doomed, but why do they not wipe out their sexual competitors first?

A western whiptail lizard (Cnemidophorus tigris). This species interbred with the little striped whiptail to produce the parthenogenetic race (Cnemidophorus neomexicanus) that now inhabits the dry river beds around the Rio Grande.

Many theories have been developed to explain this peculiar paradox, which is now one of the central problems of all biology. There is Muller's ratchet theory, which suggests that asexual creatures suffer because they cannot use sex to get rid of troublesome mutations, and so, generation after generation the wheel of time racks up mutations until the whole population is genetically inferior to the parent stock. Then there is the 'Red Queen' hypothesis, named after a passage from Lewis Carroll's *Through the Looking Glass*.

Alice looked round her in great surprise.

'Why, I do believe we've been under this tree the whole time! Everything's just as it was!'

'Of course it is,' said the Queen, 'how would you have it?'

'Well in *our* country,' said Alice, still panting a little, 'you would generally get to somewhere else if you ran very fast for a long time, as we've been doing.'

'A slow sort of country,' said the Queen. 'Now, *here*, you see, it takes all the running *you* can do, to keep in the same place. If you want to get somewhere else, you must run at least twice as fast as that!'

So the Red Queen hypothesis proposes that asexual beings die out because all their offspring are identical, but time inevitably brings changes to which the asexual creatures cannot adapt; they simply cannot run fast enough in the evolutionary race, even to stay where they are.

The 'tangled bank' hypothesis is subtly different, because it proposes that the main problem for asexual organisms is not the variation in their environment from year to year, but the variation in space, between here and a few feet away. According to this hypothesis, asexual organisms are simply unlikely to produce the variety best fitted to survive in a particular locality because they have, in effect, only one bite at the cherry, or to use a rather better analogy, they all hold the same ticket in the raffle. If one wins, they all win, but their chances are not very good. But sexual organisms produce varied progeny, each holds a different raffle ticket, and each has the same chance of coming up with the winning combination, perfectly suited to its particular patch of ground. This theory takes its name from a beautiful passage in Darwin's *The Origin of Species*.

It is interesting to contemplate an entangled bank, clothed with many plants of many kinds, with birds singing on the bushes, with various insects flitting about, and with worms crawling through the damp earth, and to reflect that these elaborately constructed forms, so different from each other, and dependent on each other in so complex a manner, have all been produced by laws acting around us.

There are more theories with more outrageous names: the 'Vicar of Bray', the 'best man', the 'hitch-hiker'. The biologists may not have solved the problem, but they have had fun trying. Unfortunately most

A virgin aphid, with her abdomen raised, gives birth to a live, asexually produced daughter.

of these hypotheses cannot explain the short-term advantages of sex, and short-term advantages there must be, simply because natural selection works primarily on individuals, not on populations. The arguments are not yet over, but for the moment at least biologists are beginning to agree that asexual beings suffer either because they cannot adapt to short-term changes in the environment, or because they cannot produce the particular variety necessary to compete for a particular patch of ground.

Either way, the asexual varieties are driven to the edges of their species range, often surviving only on the strength of their ability to colonize new habitats without a sexual partner, or, in the case of plants, to survive without their normal pollinators. Parthenogenetic animals too rely on their ability to invade and quickly fill newly created habitats; they are animal weeds. The whiptail lizard lives in the valley of the Rio Grande, where dry river beds bring sudden flash floods from the San Juan and Sangre de Christo mountains. These floods repeatedly reduce the population to a few isolated individuals who must rely on their ability to do without males in order to rebuild their numbers. Another lizard, the parthenogenetic mourning gecko is found on small islands throughout the Pacific, while most of its close relatives which are sexual live on the mainland. Virgin birth is also commonest in those insects that live in precarious habitats. The inescapable conclusion is that, like the dandelion, these creatures survive only because of their ability to recover from repeated catastrophes or single-handedly colonize offshore islands. Only this ability outweighs the long-term costs of doing without sex.

Avoiding Incest

As the history of the European aristocracy shows, too much in-breeding is not always a good thing. As long ago as the 16th century, the Spanish Habsburgs made the point quite clearly. Having amassed an enormous fortune by tactfully marrying the right people at the right time, they then tried to keep their wealth in the family by marrying each other. Within a few generations the family was extinct and the Habsburgs are now best remembered for lending their name to the strangely deformed jaw inherited by the last of their line. The genetic disease and still births that accompanied their decline were typical of inbred human groups, but the reasons for this are actually rather subtle. In all of us, some of the enormous number of genes needed as the blueprint for our bodies are almost certainly poor copies, carrying errors that prevent the proteins they design from doing their job properly. But we never notice. Each cell has two sets of each chromosome, and if one of them is capable of doing the job, the defective genes are never exposed. When close relatives mate, there is a high chance that the children will inherit a defective gene from both parents and have no functional copy at all.

In the light of this it seems extraordinary that many plants and

The two types of primrose flower

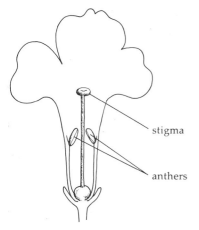

Pin-eyed flower

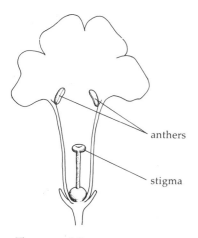

Thrum-eyed flower

The two types of primrose flower. (Top) the pin-eyed flower, with a long style which lifts the stigma above the anthers. (Above) the thrum-eyed flower, with a short style and a tuft of anthers attached to the lip where the petals fuse.

animals normally fertilize themselves. These self-fertilizers escape disaster because all the lethal genes have already been systematically removed from the population. While self-fertilization is an advantage to colonizers, plants and animals not adapted to this transient lifestyle would suffer costs that are apparently too great. Forced to inbreed, they would lose the variety that sex generates, variety that is essential if they are to keep pace with the evolution going on around them.

Most animals avoid self-fertilization by keeping the males and females as separate individuals, and some plants like the asparagus do the same. Accidental self-fertilization is perhaps most likely in plants that have hermaphrodite flowers, although the sort of tactic adopted by the primrose is a fairly effective means of preventing it. Primrose flowers are of two basic designs, which differ in the position of the anthers and the stigma. In both types the five petals join to form a narrow tube which surrounds the sexual parts of the flower. Roughly half of the flowers have the pollen-producing anthers attached half-way down this tube and the pollen-collecting stigma held at the mouth. These are called pin-eyed flowers, because the tip of the stigma looks like a pin head. In the rest of the population, the positions are reversed. The stigma is supported halfway down the tube of petals and the cluster of anthers is attached at the mouth like a tuft of wool, giving these the name of 'thrum-eyed' flowers. As long ago as 1877, Charles Darwin had already suggested that the differences between pin-eyed and thrum-eyed flowers might prevent self-fertilization. Night-flying moths, which he thought were largely responsible for pollinating the primrose, would collect pollen from pin-eyed flowers on their thorax and from thrum-eyed flowers on their abdomens. When visiting a pin-eyed plant, only thrum-eyed pollen would contact the stigma, and conversely only pollen from pin-eyed plants would contact the thrum-eyed stigma. He was right, but this is not the whole story, because primroses are also visited by many small insects, especially beetles, which scatter pollen all over the flower. What finally prevents self-pollination is that the pollen from one type of flower is unable to grow on its own type of stigma. Pin-eyed pollen can only grow on a thrum-eyed stigma and vice-versa.

Self-fertilization can be inhibited without any differences in the actual form of the flower, since the ultimate decision on whether or not the pollen which arrives will germinate and grow is made by the stigma itself. Nonetheless, the difference in flower structure may encourage cross-fertilization simply by preventing the stigma from becoming crowded with the wrong sort of pollen.

Another way to avoid the problem of the stigma being overloaded with pollen from its own flower is for the anthers and stigma to mature at different times. In the rosebay willowherb, as in many flowers, the anthers are ready first, release their pollen and then wilt before the stigma opens. With the iris it is again the structure of the flower that helps prevent self-pollination, but here the mechanism is quite different. As a bumble-bee crawls into the flower the lobes of the stigma are bent down and collect the pollen from the insect's back. As the bee

ABOVE *An anemone fish (Amphiprion clarkii) nestles in its anemone (Radianthus spp.). Two adults and several juveniles share an anemone, with the largest fish in the group taking the female role. If the female is removed or dies, the largest male changes sex.*

LEFT *'Why are they all stuck together like that?' Next time you are with a child on the beach, be prepared for the inevitable and innocent question. On the bottom of the pile of slipper limpets (Crepidula fornicata) are the females, and at the top are the younger and smaller males. For hermaphrodites, one advantage of changing sex is that it avoids the problems associated with self-fertilization.*

withdraws, the stigma lobes are folded back again, where the flower's own pollen cannot reach them.

Starting life as one sex and then changing to another is a useful way of preventing self-fertilization in the animal world too, although in animals, avoiding self-fertilization is not the only reason for changing sex. The anemone-fish *Amphiprion bicinctus* lives in the protection of a variety of sea anemones on the coral reefs of the Red Sea. They are immune to the venom of the anemone's stinging tentacles and retreat into them whenever danger threatens. A pair will remain together for several years, often accompanied by small sub-adult males, but in each group only the largest fish is female and if she is removed, the largest male changes sex and takes over. The cleaner-fish *Labroides dimidatus* performs the sex change the other way around, with all the fishes in a shoal female and only one large male. Hagfish begin life as males and then change to being females, sex in this case being only a matter of age. Slipper limpets behave in much the same way, and the stacks of shells so often found on beaches are mating piles. On the bottom are the older, bigger females and on the top are the younger, smaller males. Since sperm are easier to produce than eggs, males often mature earlier, but whether an animal begins life as a male and changes to being a female or vice versa, depends at least partly on the effective size of its social group. For anemone-fish the group is a single pair, and both fish benefit if the female is the larger since she can produce more eggs. However, for fish like the blue-headed wrasse that live in shoals, many small fish can produce more eggs than a single large one, and so both sexes benefit if the largest fish is male.

Animals like the anemone-fish and slipper limpet that begin life as one sex and then change to the other are called sequential hermaphrodites, while slugs, worms and many other hermaphrodite fishes are simultaneous hermaphrodites, that is they are both sexes at the same time, making self-fertilization at least theoretically possible. Many of these animals indulge in a reciprocal embrace, simultaneously passing sperm directly into the female duct of the other animal, so only cross-fertilization is physically possible. In externally fertilized fishes, sperm and eggs from both animals would quickly get mixed up if they mated in this way. Instead most, like the black hamlet, take it in turns to play each role. One initiates a mating bout by pushing its nose beneath its partner's tail and then swinging around so that each fish is floating with the other's tail over its head. The fish

Courtship between black hamlets. These fish are hermaphrodite, and take it in turns to play the male and female roles.

Cheetahs that have never seen the African savannah are a familiar sight in zoos today, but only ten years ago captive breeding seemed almost impossible. Then it was realized that, for cheetahs, familiarity breeds only contempt. Strangers will court and mate, but animals that have spent time together are unable to breed.

that initiates the mating bout releases its eggs, and its partner plays the role of the male and fertilizes them. Then, some time later the pair change roles; the second fish initiates a bout of courtship, and the first acts as the male. Only small batches of eggs are released each time and many changes of role are necessary before all a fish's eggs are released and fertilized.

Simply by having two sexes on different individuals, self-fertilization is easy to avoid, but self-fertilization is only the most extreme form of inbreeding. Mating with sisters or brothers has the same effect, reducing the amount of variety in the offspring and exposing harmful genes. To avoid incestuous matings is more difficult than to avoid self-fertilization, because, in order to avoid incest, animals and plants must recognize their close relatives. In plants this is done by extending the sort of genetic system that prevents the primrose from self-fertilizing. A mating between two primroses produces half thrum-eyed and half pin-eyed flowers. Half of the offspring can mate with the other half, and so the system is no guarantee against incest. Many other flowers have a similar but more complex system with not two but hundreds of 'incompatibility types', and almost all the off-spring from a cross will share at least one incompatibility marker with each other which prevents them from interbreeding.

Animals that copulate have more control over their choice of partner than plants and can prevent incest by not mating with close relatives, provided that they can tell who those close relatives actually are. Mother is usually quite easy to identify, at least in those animals where she spends some time looking after her young, and sure enough sexually mature chimpanzees and baboons can recognize their mothers and do not court or copulate with them. Pigtail monkeys and Japanese macaques can also recognize their maternal half-sisters, uncles and aunts, but learning the identity of relatives on the father's side is much more difficult, especially in primate troops where the female is promiscuous. Appearance, smell and courtship behaviour may all help mates to decide how closely related they really are. Mice rely on their sense of smell and will not court littermates, half-brothers or half-sisters. Japanese quail can tell how closely related another bird is simply by its appearance, and again avoid close relatives. Female chimpanzees often reduce the risk of mating incestuously by the simple strategy of moving to another group when they are in heat and returning to their normal troop once their period of estrus is over. In communally nesting scrub jays, it is once again the female who leaves the group in which she was born to try and establish a place in a new breeding group. If she cannot move into a new group, she returns to the territory of her birth, but will not begin to breed until her father has died or deserted. Similarly in prairie-dogs, the female is less likely to come into heat if her father is still around. Since it is the female who will become pregnant, it is no surprise that she is the more wary of the two partners whenever incest threatens to spoil her chances of raising healthy and competitive young.

Human taboos and legal controls of incest could also stem from a very primitive feeling that incest is wrong and unnatural, and it is interesting that children raised together on Israeli kibbutzim who have shared a dormitory throughout their early years very rarely marry within their group. Instead they leave the kibbutz and take a job in the city for a few years, often to return with a wife or husband. But our insight into our own taboos may have confused our understanding of sex in the natural world. Just as some plants and animals may benefit from being self-fertile, so incest too may have its advantages. If sex were only a way of shuffling the genetic information in order to get as much variety as possible, then mates should look for partners as unlike themselves as possible; but it is not. Sex is a way of producing successful offspring, and although variety is useful, very different animals that mate may be running into danger. Genes which work well together as a team may create disastrous combinations if they are mixed with a different set. It is best to mate with someone different, but not too different, and indeed many birds and mammals seem to prefer to mate with their cousins rather than with complete outsiders. Humans too choose to marry cousins in cultures where this is allowed, although as with the Habsburg monarchy, the reasons may have more to do with keeping the money in the family than unconscious drives dictated by genetics. In extreme cases it is always better to mate with a closely related animal than not to mate at all. For example, gibbons can have severe problems establishing a territory for themselves, in fact the odds are about two to one against a young male gibbon establishing a territory of his own, even with help from both parents. If the father dies, a son has little hope of setting up on his own, and instead he usually stays with his mother, who accepts him as a mate and plays her part in helping to chase away new males that may encroach on their territory. In animals where incest is common, most of the harmful recessive genes will already have been eliminated, and the only disadvantage is that the offspring are less variable. The motto perhaps is that one descendant is more varied than none at all.

chapter six

Courtship and Mating Success

A male blue-footed booby (*Sula nebouxii*) shows off his bright blue feet to a female. As a sign of appeasement the male tucks his beak into his chest during this 'parading' display, which is usually soon followed by copulation.

Ritual performances like this are an important part of courtship behaviour, especially in birds. They help potential mates to identify each other as members of the same species, and appeasement displays are important to prevent the aggression that normally follows when two animals get too close for comfort.

Primitive Courtship

For those animals which most closely resemble the first creatures to leave the sea, the scorpions and their kin, and the simple insects, courtship is not a preliminary but an essential part of the mating act.

The pseudoscorpions look much like scorpions, with two large claws (properly called pedipalps) and a flattened body, but without the stinging tail. Small and secretive, they are easily overlooked, although they are actually quite common in cracks beneath bark, among leaf litter, even beneath driftwood on the seashore. In some species there is no courtship at all and the males leave sperm packages stuck to the ground in the often vain hope that a female will find them. In other species the female is guided to the package by a pheromone, or by an intricate web of silk woven between the ground and some overhanging object, but even with these aids to navigation many sperm packages dry out and shrivel up before they are found.

Perhaps it was to avoid this waste that some pseudoscorpions developed their complex courtship dance. *Lasiochernes pilosus* is one of them. It is rarely seen, even by naturalists, for it is found only in the nests of moles. In these unpromising surroundings it lives and dies, and at some point in between, with luck it mates. Once a male has found a female he grasps her claws and tries to pull her to him. If she resists, he lets go with one claw, then circles around her, dragging her behind him. He tries once again, moving first forwards with his claws trembling, then stepping backwards again pulling the female close to him. The dance is repeated several times, as if to make sure that each knows exactly what it is doing; then the male deposits a spermatophore on the ground, which their dance has cleared of loose debris. With his claws still shaking, he once more draws the female towards him and then steps backwards. With this movement she is drawn over the sperm package and she takes it into her genital pore.

The whole process lasts over an hour, but it does make certain that the female collects the male's spermatophore and, perhaps incidentally, that the pair belong to the same species. If by chance the pair were mismatched, the dance would quickly degenerate into chaos, since each would be performing different steps.

Among brook salamanders, the same process can take even longer, but the salamanders as a group have left us with evidence of how this slow, physical courtship can evolve into a more subtle, stylized and efficient operation. Mating in brook salamanders is very physical, and there are good reasons to believe that it is similar to the type of courtship from which all other salamander courtship has evolved. Brook salamanders live in fast-flowing streams and their courtship occurs in water, exposed to all the buffeting of the current. A courting male grabs any passing salamander by its tail, which he holds firmly between his jaws. If the captured animal is a male or an unwilling female, a violent fight follows and eventually the male is forced to release his prize. But a receptive female allows the courting male to bring his vent close to hers and to stroke her with his hind legs.

Eventually, in a process that might last for days, the male manoeuvres himself into a position where he can deposit his spermatophores close to the female's vent, shoving in with his hind feet any that fail to enter immediately.

Throughout the courtship process, the male holds on to the female, since if he lets go even for a moment she will be swept away in the current. In the more placid waters inhabited by their cousins the newts, mating proceeds with less physical contact, more cooperation, and much more speed.

Like brook salamanders, smooth newts court underwater, but there the similarity ends. Instead of grabbing the female in his jaws, the male follows her attentively, pressing his head against her sides. He crosses in front of her, displaying his crest and his brightly marked and coloured flanks. Then he turns and begins lashing his tail and directing a stream of water against her snout. Tail-waving also wafts the male's scent to the female, and she soon becomes interested in his vent and begins to follow him. He stops to deposit his spermatophore on the ground, then draws her forward again. As she arrives with her vent over the spermatophore he stops her with his tail and she then presses down and collects the sperm package in her vent.

The function of courtship in scorpions, pseudoscorpions and salamanders is to transfer the sperm from male to female, but even in these creatures it has already begun to fulfil other functions as well. The tail-waving, scent-wafting and the complex dance of the smooth newt all combine to make certain that the spermatophore is transferred not just to any newt, but to one of the same species, genetically programmed to move in harmony with the dancing male.

A pair of scorpions performing their mating dance.

Recognition

What do you get if you cross a sheep with a kangaroo? Or an elephant with a mouse? This endless children's game would not be half as much fun if sheep really did mate with kangaroos, but in zoos, lions have been crossed with tigers, zebras with asses, and jaguars with leopards. Domestic hens have been mated with peacocks, and even in nature crosses between different species of duck are frequent novelties.

Many artificial hybrids are useful to humans. The mule, a cross between a horse and a donkey, has more stamina than either of its parents, and without hybrid strains of crop plants we would probably all go hungry. Wheat and maize are hybrids; so are some delicacies like the cultivated strawberry. Freak hybrids between plants are quite common in nature, since all that prevents crosses between some species is the reaction between the pollen and the stigma, and if the right sort of pollen fails to arrive, the wrong sort can sometimes make its way to the ovule. But like the mule, most hybrids are sterile, and it is a waste of reproductive effort to produce such young: they cannot reproduce themselves and yet will compete for food and space with the offspring of more conventional unions.

Selection acts to root out any animal that wastes its chances to reproduce, and so the hybrids in zoos are usually artificial creations that cannot occur naturally, the result of introducing two animals that would normally never meet. Often the parents come from different continents or different habitats, or would normally fail to interbreed because in nature they are sexually active at different seasons. Other animals fail to hybridize simply because they are physically incapable of mating. The elephant/mouse cross (from which you get big holes in your cheese) is an obvious example, but even subtle differences may prevent hybrids. The male dragonfly must grasp the female by her thorax, so that she can twist beneath him to form a 'mating wheel'. In each species, the female's thorax is slightly different and the male cannot get a grip unless the claspers on the end of his abdomen fit each bump and hollow precisely; even closely related species may be incapable of hybridizing because they are physically incompatible.

Animals which live in the same areas and are physically capable of interbreeding usually cannot produce viable offspring. Either the sperm die inside the female before reaching the egg or, as with crosses between goats and sheep, the egg is fertilized but the embryo soon aborts. In practice this is only the last line of defence against a futile conception and most animals save time, energy and gametes by preventing such a mistake before it even begins.

Advertising signals act as the first barrier to mistaken matings, and the more complex and detailed the advertisement, the less attractive it will be to animals of the wrong species. The flashing Morse code of a firefly precisely identifies the caller at the same moment that it advertises his presence, and the delicately choreographed dance of the mayfly is unmistakable to a female sitting in the hedge nearby. The clearest and most conclusive evidence that advertising signals play an

The dewlap of Anolis lizards may be important in helping the many species in this group to tell each other apart. Where different species share a common habitat, the differences in size and colour of the dewlap are sometimes exaggerated, even though away from the boundaries the dewlap of both species is quite similar.

important role in preventing hybridization comes from Australia. Here live two tree-frogs: Ewing's tree-frog (*Hyla ewingi*) which occupies an area extending westwards along the coast from Melbourne, and its close relative *Hyla verreauxi*, which is more common along the coast from Melbourne eastwards. The advertising call of both frogs is a very similar, rapid trill, although the call of the Ewing's tree-frog is perhaps a little slower. But in the area around Melbourne, the ranges of the two species overlap and their calls are different. Here, the trill of Ewing's tree-frog is much slower and the call of *H. verreauxi* is much faster, and the females that live in this area prefer these calls to the 'normal' calls of their cousins from the country. The Melbourne dialects help the females to avoid creating infertile hybrids.

Making certain that her mate is the correct species is important for the female tree-frog because, if she makes a mistake, she wastes all her eggs producing young that have little chance of survival. For the male, things are not so bad. Most of his effort goes into calling for the female, only a little into actually producing sperm, and he can mate many times. Consequently he has no need to be very choosey. For the male jumping spider, it is very different. His mate is a potential predator and he must take special care to make certain that she is the right species and that she understands his intentions. So he performs a zig-zag dance in front of her, raising his front legs and twitching his palps. If she is receptive and recognizes his display she will answer with a leg-waving display of her own and then crouch in front of him. Only when all the preliminaries have been correctly performed will he come forward to mate.

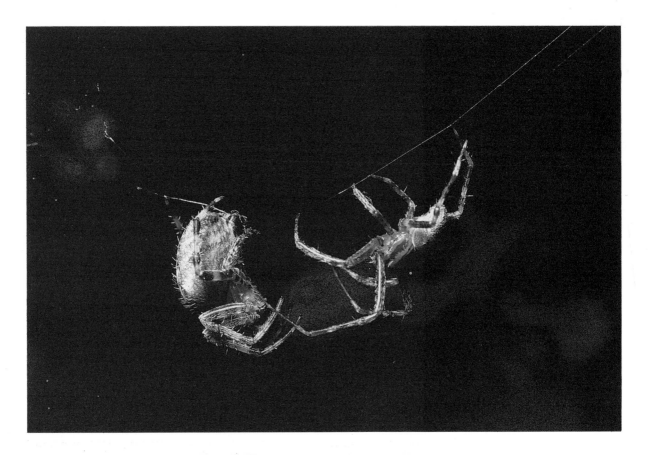

ABOVE *The male common garden spider has attached a mating line to the female's web and encouraged her to move on to it. Now he can inseminate her without running such risks of being eaten.*

LEFT *The male praying mantis was not so lucky.*

Male orbweb spiders are even more at risk. Their partners are often larger than themselves and are normally indiscriminate killers, attacking anything that touches their web. As a prelude to mating, males announce their intentions by plucking at the silken threads with a species-specific rhythm. A mistake in this rhythm invites more than artistic criticism, though by remaining at the edge of the web the male gives himself a reasonable chance of escape. Once the male is confident that his messages have been received and understood, he attaches a mating line to the web. By plucking the line he encourages the female to move on to it and hang from it so that he can rush in and deliver his syringe full of sperm.

How to avoid being eaten by the female is a problem for most spiders. Some crab-spiders first tie their mate down with ropes of silk, while the tarantula takes no chances and holds the female's jaws apart with special hooks on his front legs. The male praying mantis faces much the same danger from his mate. She is quick and occasionally deadly, although even a headless male that has paid dearly for his poorly executed courtship can sometimes rely on his reflexes to bring the mating to a successful climax. Contrary to the popular myth, the male is rarely killed in nature. In some species he relies on stealth, approaching the female from behind and jumping quickly onto her back, tucking his head behind hers to avoid her clutching forelegs. Males of other species have brightly coloured limbs which are used to pass semaphore signals to the females. The small Indian mantis (*Ephestiasula amoena*) begins its courtship of a female by slowly extending each foreleg in turn, showing off their distinctive black, red and white patterns and attracting her attention by quickly flicking his feet. The patterns of closely related species are strikingly different and the partners identify each other through such displays before mating.

Male butterflies are in no danger of being attacked by their mates, but some species have serious difficulties when it comes to identifying the correct partner. Adult butterflies often carry poisons which they collected in their days as caterpillars and with which they surprise any bird that attacks them. Milkweed, the larval foodplant of the African queen (*Danaus chrysippus*) contains the cardiac glycosides calactin and calotropin, and one peck is enough for any bird to learn that these conspicuous, brightly coloured butterflies are bad news. Over the years, less well-protected butterflies have evolved colours and patterns that precisely mimic those of their poisonous models. The mimics, like the female *Hypolimnas missipus,* are often painstaking copies, identical down to the last detail, brightly but fraudulently advertising their distastefulness.

This confuses the predators, but it also confuses any male that is searching for a mate. Once again it is through courtship that the species sort themselves out. The male hypolimnas selects a particular stone, stem or patch of ground where he sits and waits, flying at anything that passes, especially if it is large and orange and promises to be a female. Once he has found something that looks about right, he flies along a few centimetres beneath it. If it is indeed a female

The larva of the African queen butterfly (Danaus chrysippus) feeds on milkweed plants, cleverly storing the poisons that the plants manufacture for their own protection, to defend itself against predators. The butterfly (left) advertises its distastefulness with bright colours, which are copied in detail by the unrelated female Hypolimnas missipus. The male hypolimnas (right) looks identical to both his mate and the African queen with his wings folded, but as they open he reveals himself to be a different species, which helps the female to select the correct mate.

hypolimnas, she recognizes this subtle approach and the male's completely distinctive blue-and-white upper wings, and settles on the ground, and the male then pushes beneath her and twists his abdomen up in order to mate.

These courtship movements mean nothing to the female African queen, who will simply ignore a courting male hypolimnas flying beneath her. She recognizes only a male that beats her about the antennae with his abdomen as she flies along or sits quietly on a stem. From the tip of his abdomen the male African queen pokes out two small brushes which contain a pheromone, a close-acting scent signal that identifies him unmistakably as the correct species. The female hypolimnas simply fly away when treated to this performance, but female African queens are literally intoxicated. So by a combination of scent and behaviour, the two species can tell each other apart and infertile cross-matings rarely, if ever, occur.

Ritual

In the days when people cut off each other's heads in public, a proffered handshake meant something like, 'Look, I have no sword and I hope very much that you too are unarmed.' Nowadays, when businessmen slaughter each other only metaphorically and in the decent privacy of their own boardrooms, the handshake carries a message quite different from its original purpose. It means something like, 'Hello, this is me; who are you, shall we talk?' And yet the gesture is the same and still performed with the sword-hand, even though the ritual greeting now has a completely different meaning.

Almost any sort of behaviour can be ritualized; but much ritual courtship behaviour in animals seems to stem from frustration. Sit a cat beneath a bird-table and all around, well out of range, perch the birds, each one acting out bits of its courtship repertoire. The food and the cat give them completely opposing motivations, and confused by the conflict they neither approach nor take flight but do something else instead. They preen themselves, or wipe their beaks or hop up and down anxiously.

Importantly, not only do they all do something else, they all do something different, and natural selection has seized on these differences in behaviour to help mates recognize that each is the correct species. Early in evolutionary history a male duck, unable to resolve the conflicting demands of his urge to mate and his fear of approaching too close to a female, must have turned in frustration to preen himself. Perhaps the female felt this obsessive preening to be a mark of the family and accepted him as a mate. From this simple beginning arose a whole range of complex preening rituals. Instead of actually preening, the drakes now need only turn to point at a brightly

Mandarin ducks and a tree peony. An 18th-century Japanese fan print captures the courtship display of the male quite accurately.

A village weaverbird displaying beneath his nest.

coloured wing feather or a distinctive patch on the tail, and their movements have become slow and deliberate, making their intent quite unmistakable. The gaudy mandarin drake erects his crest, touches the water with his beak and then turns to point at the gorgeous orange fin-feathers that stick up from his tail, lifting those that are on the side towards the female to show off briefly the contrasting metallic blue of the outer vane. The drake no longer needs to preen; he simply goes through the motions, now emphasized by the striking colours and the feathers which are so exaggerated that he hardly needs to stretch in order to reach them.

Touching the water with his beak is also a ritual. Two ducks that meet on a lake for the first time almost invariable drink, so long as they are on neutral territory. This happens so predictably that it cannot be coincidence, but must be a sign of peace in the ducks' gestural vocabulary. In courtship, the sign has become ritualized, and in some species the duck does not even touch the water, although the action is still unmistakable. Taken together, the ritual drinking and the ritual preening of the mandarin drake say simply, 'I am a mandarin drake and I want to mate: now.'

The frustrated ancestors of the zebra finches must have stopped not to preen nor drink, but to wipe their beaks. Courtship between zebra finches begins with the male singing his rather squeaky song and dancing towards the female. His dance is stylized, and with each hop he swings his head and tail through a wide arc and swaps his feet on the perch to face in the opposite direction. In between hops he pauses to wipe his beak; except that once again the movement has become a ritual. Often his beak will not touch the branch, and instead of the careful wiping it would get if it were really dirty, the courtship version is simply a couple of quick shakes in the air.

The basic conflict between mating and fleeing from a partner who is getting too close for comfort has been resolved rather differently by the black-headed gull. These small and fragile-looking gulls are almost as quarrelsome as their larger relatives, and as if to make up for their frail build, their threatening stare is reinforced by a dark-brown face-mask. A bird wanting to avoid trouble simply turns his head to one side, and this has become part of the black-headed gull's courtship routine. Instead of staring deep into each other's eyes, the birds put their partners at ease by looking the other way.

South of the Sahara, the male African village weaverbird is similarly handicapped by black feathers on his head and back which are fluffed up in an aggressive threat display. When trying to attract a female to his nest, the male does his best not to look threatening. He hangs upside down near his nest, hiding his black back from the female but flapping his wings and fanning his tail to emphasize his yellow feathers. It is all an attempt to avoid giving the wrong message; like the black-headed gull, he seems intent on saying, 'I am not a threat, I only want to mate.'

Male fiddler crabs do not give unambiguous signals, but rely on the female to interpret their displays according to her mood. The waving of the male's oversized claw serves to keep other males away and at the same time to attract females to his burrow in the tidal mudflats. For this to be an effective means of courtship, the behaviour of the female must change completely once she becomes receptive, and simply by calling the male's bluff and approaching his burrow she announces that she is ready to mate.

The male fiddler crab quickly responds to the female's new behaviour; but bullheads are rather slow to get the message, as their name might almost imply. The bullhead is a small fish, and like the stickleback the male protects the eggs in a nest that is hollowed out beneath a stone or rock. The nest is prepared single-handedly by the male, who either digs with his mouth or swims beneath the rock to shoot out a current of water and sand by rapidly beating his tail. Once he has excavated his nest, he waits at its entrance and defends his new territory against other males. Fish that stray too close are chased and bitten, and during these displays the head of the attacker may change colour, turning a deep black. Usually other fish flee instantly, but a ripe female shows no fear at all if she receives the same treatment, which now becomes a courtship bite. Her response is to swim into the nest, where she will mate and lay her eggs.

The claw-waving display of the fiddler crab may have evolved because crabs see movement better than form, and female crabs perhaps originally picked out the males from their surroundings as they moved their claws to feed. The females have selected males with larger and larger claws, and now the male's enlarged claw is useless for feeding, yet he must still make the ritualized feeding movement if he is to attract a female.

Great crested grebes seem to do almost everything together, but when they have been separated and then reunite, they perform the weed dance shown here. Each bird grabs a beakful of nesting material and rises almost vertically in the water. The display may have begun as displacement nest-building behaviour, but has now become an integral part of the grebe's courtship behaviour.

ABOVE *The courtship display of the male Barrow's goldeneye. This display probably had its beginnings as an escape movement but the nervous bird with its head up and about to leave must eventually have mated, and the display has now become a part of the courtship ritual.*

In birds, the temptation to escape can itself be ritualized, the message of an upward-pointing beak being quite clearly, 'I feel like getting out of here; I am even more worried about this than you are.' This has become an essential part of the courtship between boobies, large seabirds in the pelican family with a rich repertoire of gestures. The male brown booby simply raises his beak to the sky, keeping his wings folded; but in other boobies the display is more complex. The white booby opens his wings as well as 'sky-pointing', and in the Peruvian booby the wings are twisted so that their upper surface points towards the female. The ritual reaches its climax in the blue-footed booby, where the wings are twisted with the beak and the tail pointed skywards, and uniquely the display is mutual, with the female performing the same gestures.

Interestingly, in the closely related gannets, the display serves a different function. The closely packed gannet colony is a dangerous place for eggs or young birds left alone, even for a moment, because adults will not hesitate to kill unguarded chicks, and before leaving the nest a gannet always performs the sky-pointing display to make it clear that its partner should stay behind. If both birds feel the same urge at the same time the display is mutual and will continue until one or the other gives in and lets its partner escape for a while from the duties of protecting the nest.

chapter seven

The Male View

Males produce large numbers of sperm, which gives them the potential to inseminate many partners, and so they often find themselves competing with each other for access to the same female. Male Siamese fighting fish, as their name implies, simply fight to decide who mates with the female. However, many of the strategies that males employ are much more subtle.

Fighting

James Bond's evil adversary Dr No kept Siamese fighting fish as pets. Put these beautiful creatures into a small aquarium together and they will fight to the death, nicely symbolizing the mindless machismo essential to the plot of the film. Why do animals fight? At best the loss of a leg, a broken wing or a deep cut will ruin their chances of mating that season. At worst the victim will die of starvation or infection. One study of musk-oxen in Canada's Northwest Territories found that up to a tenth of all the bulls die each year during the rut. These bulls fight by charging each other head to head, colliding with a sickening crunch that makes human onlookers wince and hold their ears. If either bull is stunned by the impact (and this often happens) the other will use the temporary advantage to gore his rival's flank. Dead and dying bulls with gore wounds to their ribs and lungs and severe internal injuries are a sad but common sight throughout the month of August when the rut is at its height. Male narwhals use their lethal-looking tusk for fighting, and many adult males have a broken tusk and scars on their heads as constant reminders of previous battles; some even have bits of others' tusks embedded in their jaws. It is not only large animals that engage in this seemingly pointless violence. Male dragonflies quite frequently drown each other in territorial disputes, and male stag beetles can inflict serious damage on their rivals with their outsized pincers. Size makes no difference, but big or small it is usually the males that fight and what they fight over is females.

BELOW LEFT Unlikely though it may seem, stag beetles really do this to each other. After squeezing him hard and perhaps smacking his head against the branch, the victor will throw the loser to the ground.

BELOW RIGHT Dall rams butting heads. Males judge each other on the size of their horns, and only animals with similar-sized weapons resort to combat to decide who will mate.

Females rarely get involved in these conflicts simply because they have no need to. A female can increase her reproductive success by laying more eggs and in order to do this she needs to eat more, or turn her food into eggs more efficiently. Having more males chasing after her will not help her at all; in fact they will probably just get in the way. A single male produces thousands of sperm at each mating, so mating twice is just a waste of time for most females. For males, things are very different. There are comparatively few male animals that can help their young in any way once the female's eggs have been fertilized, and for these males the best hope for leaving a thriving family behind is to mate as often as they can. With all the males trying to mate with all the females and all the females needing to mate only once, confict between males for access to females is inevitable, a conflict acted out not only between the imposing and well-armed highland stags, but between male fishes, male birds and even male bees.

On warm April mornings the sand dunes of Europe hum with the sound of mining bees (*Colletes daviesanus*), patrolling in search of females. As a female begins to emerge from her pupa beneath the sand, she emits a pheromone which attracts the males who help dig her out. Once in the open, her smell attracts males like flies to dead meat. Thirty or forty bees pile together in a seething buzzing bundle, which rolls down the dunes as each scrambles to get to the middle and mate with the female. Injury to some of the males is inevitable, but 'gentlemanly' bees that step aside and escape the risk do not get to mate and cannot pass on their genes. The females mate only once, and

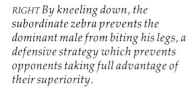

RIGHT By kneeling down, the subordinate zebra prevents the dominant male from biting his legs, a defensive strategy which prevents opponents taking full advantage of their superiority.

in this species at least, grabbing them as they emerge is the only way that the males can hope to find a virgin.

For these male colletes bees, there is no realistic alternative but joining in the mating bundles and risking injury. The mating behaviour of the digger bee (*Centris pallida*) from the deserts of the south-western United States is even more aggressive. They too search for and dig out females, but they also try to dispose of potential competitors before the female that they are all waiting for has emerged. The female sometimes escapes from her burrow while the males are busy grappling with each other, and so fighting at a burrow site is not the last chance to ensure success for male centris bees. Males can also search out females away from their burrows, and instead of trying to oust the large males, small males concentrate their efforts on searching around flowers for unmated females.

Competition for females need not result in a fight. In many species, males have evolved elaborate defences, and attacks that are effectively neutralized are just a waste of effort. Small bull rhinos will run shoulder to shoulder with larger opponents, denying them the opportunity to charge their flank. A dog or wolf getting the worst of a fight will try to bite the muzzle of the dominant animal and so protect itself from a more serious bite on the neck. Defensive strategies effectively make fighting more costly and time-consuming for the aggressors. Even for a dominant male, attacking still carries with it an element of risk; he may miss his footing as he charges, or he may wound his adversary and incite a furious and deadly counter-attack.

Because there is no certainty that the best male will win, most animals do not begin their confrontations by fighting seriously. For both parties it is often better to establish a likely winner through a formal contest and then abide by the decision that is reached. Such displays are common in the animal kingdom. Male vipers often perform a ritual combat, twisting around one another, each trying to force the other's head to the ground. The loser is momentarily pinned down and then makes off into the undergrowth. In the extreme north of Europe, the female vipers are only fertile in alternate years and so there is intense competition between the males, yet the rules of the ritual display are apparently never broken. Should the weaker male turn and bite his opponent he would almost certainly be bitten in return, so there is no sense in escalating the conflict.

Male common toads also have a formal display to help them decide who will mate with a female. Males again outnumber females, this time because the females stay at the pond only long enough to mate and lay their eggs. The males spend much longer at the pond, waiting throughout the breeding season, jumping on any female that approaches. By the time the female reaches the pond, she will almost certainly have a male on her back. Once there, the scrummaging begins as unattached males kick and pull at the pairs, trying to dislodge the male in residence and take his place. He replies by kicking out with his hind legs and muttering soft croaks. A deep bass croak tells the attacker that the toad in the saddle is a big one and that the

ABOVE *Two male adders sparring, each trying to push the other to the ground.*

OPPOSITE ABOVE *During the rut, red deer stags roar continuously, day and night.*

OPPOSITE BELOW *The contest between male elephant seals is fierce, but the reward is a harem of twenty or more females.*

Red kangaroos fighting. Red kangaroos do not hold a territory, and fights occur only when a male is directly challenged for the right to mate with a female.

attack is probably futile. A squeaky alto croak betrays a small male and a large attacker redoubles his efforts to take over the mating position on the female. The prize is valuable, and despite the code of conduct, fights may go on for hours, especially if two contestants are closely matched. By croaking at each other, the toads at least manage to avoid wasting energy on completely futile squabbling.

The greater the rewards, the more risks a male will take to secure them; and nowhere are the rewards for males greater than in those animals where the male holds a harem. Landseer doubtless knew all about the mating habits of the red deer when he painted *The Monarch of the Glen*, and so too did the Victorian paterfamilias who hung a print over the fireplace, for the monarch of the glen has things his own way at the expense of lesser males.

In spring and summer, the stags keep apart from the hinds, feeding and fattening, and by early autumn they are in peak condition; the prime males proudly bear the magnificent antlers that they have been growing throughout the summer. As the hinds come into season, the rut begins, and the glens echo to the clash of weapons and the bellowing roars, or so Landseer's painting implies. Actually the monarch who controls a harem is desperately trying to hold on to his party of hinds (and the bigger the party the better). He has to check whether or not they are in season, mate with them, proclaim his territory, and continually chase away other stags. He has little time to eat and less time to sleep. Most disputes between stags are settled by mutual display, which helps the animals to decide who is more likely to win. Firstly the stags announce their fighting fitness to all challengers by roaring every thirty seconds throughout the day and night. Challenged by the roar of another stag, the harem-holder responds by roaring more often, beginning a slanging match with his challenger that may last an hour. At the climax, both males may be roaring once every ten seconds. This may decide the outcome of the confrontation, but if the two stags are well matched, they will go on to the next stage of the contest. The rivals march together across the heather, about 10 metres (30 feet) apart, apparently sizing each other up. This 'parallel walk' may go on for thirty minutes, or for only a few seconds, and once again it may result in the challenger withdrawing. Sometimes a fight is the only way to settle the matter and the stags turn and clash head to head, grappling with their antlers. These fights are not displays but real tussles, in which one or other of the animals may lose an eye or break a leg, but if the contestants are closely matched and a large harem is at stake, the risk is worthwhile.

The stag's roaring and his large antlers advertise his social status, but these outward symbols alone are not enough to ensure dominance and must be backed up with the appropriate behaviour. 'Cheats' could possibly evolve, creatures who displayed the signs of a dominant animal while actually being weak and feeble, but their bluff would soon be called. The appearance of cheats would no doubt soon be followed by the evolution of 'vandals' who would challenge everyone physically and ignore the social conventions. Possibly the regular and damaging fights of the Canadian musk-ox represent exactly this stage in the evolution of their behaviour. For a combat display to be effective and prevent the appearance of cheats and vandals, the advertisements must be honest, legal and truthful. The toad's deep croak, the stag's continuous roaring, and the massive horns of the mountain sheep have probably been selected as combat displays because they are difficult for inferior males to imitate; they are related directly to an animal's size, physical health and fighting prowess.

Bribery and Extortion

Towards the end of the summer throughout the woodlands of Europe, speckled wood butterflies fight for their place in the sun. The males spiral together in the air beating their wings against each other to defend sunspots against intruders. Sunspots are a valuable commodity because this is where the newly emerged virgin females will come to warm themselves. Although the fight is over females, the winner is not the strongest nor the most agile male, but the male originally sitting in the patch of sunlight. It is as if the challenger is saying, 'Terribly sorry, I had no idea you were here, please take all the females for yourself.' How can such selflessness survive if only the most determined males reproduce and pass on their genes?

Fitness means much more than the ability to beat up all challengers. Many creatures could not survive without cooperating either with others of the same species, or even by forming close relationships with members of other species. Although competition is one essential feature of Darwin's theory of evolution, nature is not always 'red in tooth and claw'. 'The survival of the fittest' is in many ways an unfortunate phrase, since being fit means more than being strong and

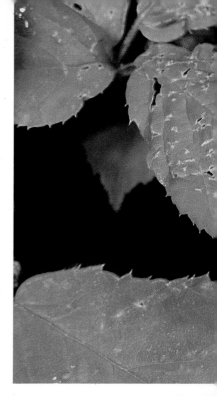

healthy. For the male speckled wood butterfly, being fit also means knowing exactly when to back down.

In most woods there are many sunspots, and as the sun moves across the sky they shift and change, appear and disappear. Although females must sit in the sun to warm themselves, no particular spot is much better than any other, and so for the male there is no great advantage in occupying any particular patch. To agree the outcome of a confrontation by some simple, almost arbitrary rule is far better than to fight, since even between butterflies, fighting can be a serious business. Both combatants may lose wing scales or even have their fragile wings torn by their opponent's blows. In the dense conifer forests of Sweden, where little sunlight penetrates as far as the ground, fights are very real, and only the largest males manage to hold sunspot territories. In very open woods with many sunspots, the males abandon their territorial strategy and fly around the wood searching for females. But in the dappled light of the typical European oak woodland, the males defend their sunspots according to the simple rule that the resident always wins, and long damaging fights occur only when the butterflies are confused about who was first to arrive.

The convention that the owner always wins (charmingly called 'the bourgeois convention' by biologists) is a useful way of settling disputes. Animals often retain their territory in exactly this way, fiercely attacking an intruder, but fleeing should they encounter another animal when they are outside their own territory. Moreover, setting up the boundaries can involve real aggression, since they are so important. Once the males have established their territory, they will use it in order to bribe females into mating with them.

The exact nature of the bribe depends on what the female most needs in order to raise her young. Often, as in the case of many birds, the territory must contain a food supply large enough to feed the whole family. Tawny owls, for instance, feed largely on wood mice and bank voles during the early part of the breeding season, and a pair will attempt to breed only in years in which their territory promises enough food to raise the young. Male dragonflies guard glistening patches of weed and mud close to the surface of their pond, on which females will lay their eggs once the male has mated with them. For the yellow-bellied marmot, a rodent from the Rocky Mountains, the male who attracts most females is the one whose territory holds the best burrow site. Female lark buntings can be forced to mate with a polygamous male if his territory contains trees whose shade will protect the nest. The second female gets no help at all from her mate, but she will copulate with him and nest in his territory even though there are other, unmated males nearby who would help to raise the brood. Shade is all-important to the young since the main cause of infant mortality in the sun-baked grasslands of South Dakota is desiccation. Suitable nest sites, well protected from predators, are the inducement that male red-winged blackbirds offer to their females, and often the female will choose to join an already mated male if his offer is better than that of his unattached rivals.

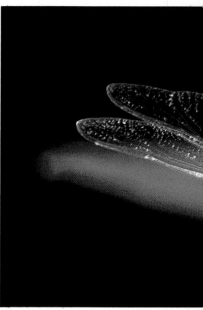

TOP *A male speckled wood butterfly sits waiting in a sunspot.*

ABOVE *A displaying dragonfly proclaims his territory with an aggressive tail-up display.*

RIGHT A tawny owl holds a woodmouse in its claw. The availability of mice and voles in a territory determines whether or not the female will attempt to breed.

By guarding a bee's nest, the orange-rumped honeyguide has the opportunity to mate with almost all the females in the area. Honeyguides are a small group of birds which lay their eggs in other birds' nests, just as cuckoos do, and so neither males nor females make any direct contribution to raising the young once the eggs are laid. Honeyguides take their name from their endearing habit of leading animals, and particularly people, to the nests of honey-bees. In many areas honeyguides have built up a mutual understanding with the local people, who follow the birds' chattering song to a nest, tear apart the tree in which it is hidden and collect most of the honey, leaving a little of the comb for their guide.

The Asian orange-rumped honeyguide, unlike many of its African relatives, has no need for human help, for the nests of the wild giant honey-bees on whose honey and wax it feeds are hung from the exposed faces of steep cliffs. A male defends his bees' nest against poaching by other males, not just through the breeding season, but throughout the year. Only his mates and their young are allowed to feed. Excluded males sit at the edge of a nest-owner's territory and try to mate with passing females (who usually struggle to free themselves). For the male that guards the bees' nest, the females will do anything; they must, since wax and honey are an important part of their diet. One male, watched for a breeding season, succeeded in mating with more than eighteen females, perhaps as many as twenty-eight, but the numbers are uncertain since some of his mates were not ringed and could not be identified as individuals. The females acquiesce in this arrangement, not simply because they cannot get food elsewhere; they can also be sure that they are mating with the toughest, most dominant male in the area and passing on his genes to their young.

On the island of Dominica in the Gulf of Mexico, female humming-birds must also give sexual favours to the males, this time in return for being allowed to feed at the flowers of banana plants. The males will chase off intruders into their patch, but persistent females are allowed to feed. The birds then display to each other, hovering in front of their partner, bill raised to show off the iridescent throat patch which identifies them as purple-throated Carib humming-birds. Even outside the breeding season when the sexual organs of both birds are degenerate and not producing eggs or sperm, they court and copulate. The female is allowed to collect food in return and, perhaps, gets into the habit of feeding in the male's territory and allowing him to mate with her. Later, when she is fertile, the male reaps his reward.

Sneaky Tactics

The male often has a frustrating life. He is either harassed by dominant stags protecting their harems, or spurned by female honeyguides because he cannot offer them food. For some it will only be a matter of time before they are strong enough and wise enough to depose the harem-master or to defend a bees' nest of their own, but others may never mate at all, a fate that is unlikely to befall many females. Although these subordinate males are incapable of overthrowing their oppressors legitimately, there are many other, more devious routes by which they can achieve their ends. Red deer stags might gain little by advertising a prowess that they cannot live up to, but this is not the only way to beat the system. Many red deer populations also contain hummels, sexually mature males that fail to grow antlers at all, a trait which survives despite the efforts of game wardens to eliminate these 'inferior' animals. In order for the trait to survive, these animals must mate, and yet without weapons they cannot possibly hold harems, and presumably they sneak quick copulations with hinds while the dominant stag is busy roaring, fighting or mating elsewhere in his harem.

Sneaky tactics are common in nature. The Gila topminnow was once a common fish in the tributaries of the Gila river in New Mexico. The jet black males defend small territories about half a metre square, chasing away other males and mating with females that wander into the territory. The female bears live young within her body, so the male must fertilize the eggs internally. He courts the female by swimming in front of her with his head tilted upwards and his dorsal fin flattened, and then nibbles at her before thrusting his anal fin into her vent. Small males cannot outfight large males for territory, so they adopt a different strategy. Like the females they remain light in colour, and so avoid being constantly pestered by the territorial males. This allows them to move with rather more freedom through the territories of the dominant males, though even the light-coloured males cannot completely avoid being chased by territory holders. Nor can they encourage females to stop swimming by courting them; in fact females that spot a light coloured male creeping up on them will often make off at speed. To mate successfully, the small males must adopt a low profile approach, rushing the female with none of the preliminary nibbling or courtship. Despite their small size, the anal fins of the non-territorial males are almost as long as the fins of the larger, dominant males, and this helps them surprise the females, although their mating thrusts are usually fleeting. These light-coloured males are rejected by the females if they are spotted in time, and so get less opportunities to mate in any one season, but they make up for this by maturing earlier and waste less time and energy fighting.

Similar sneaky tactics are used by male salmon. While some Atlantic salmon spend years feeding at sea so that on their return they weigh around 20 kilograms (40 or 50 lb), others move back into the river after only a year, when they are still mere waifs weighing only a few pounds. These grilse ('jacks' if they are chinook or sockeye salmon) are precocious males that slip alongside the large females as they are mating and release their sperm at the same moment as her intended partner on the other side.

Female tiger salamanders (*Ambystoma tigrinum*) follow the male as he deposits his spermatophores on the floor of the breeding pond,

playing out a complex mating sequence quite similar to that of the smooth newt described earlier. During the tail-nudging walk, a male relies completely on touch to keep track of the female following him, and this allows other males to sneak in between the pair unnoticed. The first male assumes he is still leading the female, and the second male follows the first male as if he were indeed a female, and leads the third, the real female, behind him. As the first male sticks his spermatophore to the bed of the pond, the trio stops. When he has finished, they move off again, and when the second male arrives over the spermatophore, he in turn stops and sticks one of his own on top. This arouses no suspicion in the first male, since the female he assumes he is leading would also stop at this point to collect his sperm package. The first male often produces another spermatophore at this point, and the trio move off once again. A little further along, the real female stops to begin collecting the sperm packages, but only picks up those of the second male, which of course are on the top. By the time the first male turns around to see what has happened, it is too late.

The male tiger salamander does his best to avoid this problem by pushing the female away from other males before he begins courting, shoving her through the water with his snout to a quiet corner of the pond where he is less likely to be interfered with.

Similar problems beset those springtails and pseudoscorpions that leave spermatophores lying around for females to find. A male that finds another male's sperm package may either deposit one of his own on top of it, or in some cases will attack it with his claws, bending it over so that it is useless. This may sound like nothing more than sour grapes, but once again the behaviour improves the male's chances of mating, since the fewer rival spermatophores left lying around, the more chance there is of fertilizing an unmated female.

Cramping the style of other males is also productive for fireflies.

Mallards mating. Even the cooperative mating seen here looks aggressive, but the female is helping her mate by lifting her tail so that he can bring his vent against hers. Forced copulations almost invariably take place on land, since on water an uwilling female can escape by diving.

When a male firefly (*P. macdermotti*) observes a male-female dialogue, he often quickly inserts a flash into the pattern of his rival, disrupting his timing and causing the exchange to start again, sometimes even confusing the female so much that she stops answering. In much the same way, some New Guinea grasshoppers insert 'Bronx cheers' into the elaborate and carefully constructed courtship songs of rivals; but it is rare that the motivation for this behaviour is completely spiteful. Messing up the courtship of rivals, like any other activity, takes time and energy and also attracts predators and so carries a risk. Usually the risk is not justified unless the male has a good chance of moving in and mating himself, since the male gains little by cutting out one competitor. In special circumstances, just to spoil a rival's chances can indeed be worthwhile. In the intestines of rats lives an internal parasite, the thorny-headed worm. The males of these tiny creatures possess a special 'cement gland' that produces a secretion which plugs the genital pore of a mated female, preventing other males from fertilizing her. As we shall see in the next section, this is a common tactic in the animal kingdom, but the male thorny-headed worms go a step further. They do not restrict their attentions to females; they also cut down on the prospective competition by slamming a mating plug into the reproductive tract of other males, effectively sterilizing them.

If males can inseminate a fertile female and do this at the expense of other males, so much the better. As well as increasing their own reproductive success, they cut down on the competition that their offspring will face. Bedbugs, for example, have evolved a peculiar method of mating, in which the male injects sperm into the female through her body wall and into her blood. Quite how this strange method of insemination has come about is a mystery, but the evolution of a male organ capable of piercing the female's body has had one very bizarre consequence. Male bedbugs now improve their reproductive performance by mating other males (presumably against their will) and injecting their sperm. This is not merely a case of mistaken identity, nor a waste of effort. The sperm migrate to the testes of the recipient male, who cannot help but pass them on when he in turn mates with a female.

Many sneaky tactics deny the female any freedom in her choice of mate. Forced copulations perpetrated by animals like the small male topminnows have sometimes been called rapes even by respectable biologists who know better. However, the word 'rape' implies so much more than mating against the female's will that it is confusing, even dangerous since it might be mistaken to imply that rape is a 'natural' phenomenon in humans.

Male mallards protect their mates early in the season, but once the female has laid her clutch of eggs, the males desert their mates and join together in groups, chasing after and forcing themselves on unwilling females. Such chases are a familiar sight in parks, where a group of males will fly after a single female and try to force her to land. Once on the ground, the female resists mounting attempts by shifting her tail from side to side, trying to prevent the male from introducing his

Orangutans usually form temporary pairs while the female is receptive. The female often initiates copulation herself, signalling her readiness to mate by extravagantly grooming the male, rubbing his genitals, or pressing her genitals against him. A male that has not formed a 'consortship' will sometimes try to force himself on a female, and the ensuing fights are occasionally protracted and violent, with the female trying to slap and bite the male throughout his attempt to copulate.

phallus. If the female's mate is nearby, he will rush to her defence, but the behaviour survives so some males must occasionally mate successfully.

Even insects will attempt forced copulations if prevented from mating according to the rules. A male scorpion fly that cannot successfully court his partner will rush at a passing female and try to grab her with pincers on the end of his abdomen. If he succeeds, he slowly adjusts his position so that he can grasp her wing in a clamp on his back specially designed for the purpose. He can then release the grip of his pincers, and with them he begins trying to grasp the abdomen of the struggling female, who constantly twists her body in an attempt to keep it out of reach of the male. Few of these forced copulation attempts succeed, and the struggle is in sharp contrast to the gentle, cooperative behaviour which characterizes mating that has been preceded by courtship. But once again the occasional success makes the strategy worth trying when all else has failed.

Some of the tricks used by males are so devious, and they seem to develop so many new ways to beat the system, that until recently they were dismissed as examples of aberrant and inappropriate male behaviour that could not serve any useful function. Even now it is often hard to believe that these lowly animals are actually capable of the complicated ruses that we are crediting them with. These discoveries about dirty tricks in the animal world have surprised and even upset some people, like the woman arrested in England for killing all the drakes on a village pond because she had heard of their ungentlemanly behaviour. However, natural selection passes no moral judgments, and the only restraint on an animal's behaviour is that it must be economical and effective.

Protecting the Investment

Even in the age of test-tube babies and surrogate mothers it is still impossible for a doctor to prove beyond doubt who is the father of a child. If determining paternity is difficult with human beings, it is almost impossible with animals. Many an animal breeder, excitedly awaiting the birth of the next Cruft's champion Alsation or prize-winning Siamese has stepped back in horror as out into the daylight has popped not the expected pedigree pet but a scruffy mongrel. Often even the mother herself seems to feign surprise, as if she cannot imagine how the dreadful deed has been done. Just a few moments out of sight during the crucial period of estrus is all that it takes for a second male to make his contribution to the litter, a problem that not only worries animal breeders but the animals themselves. A male invests time and energy in mating with a female and if she mates again his offspring will have to compete for her attention with the progeny of other males.

Males of many species stuff a plug into the female as they mate that prevents others from fertilizing her. The ejaculation of male mosquitoes hardens into a stiff, waxy jelly, which subsequent suitors cannot easily penetrate, and many male butterflies secrete a special plug after they have transferred their spermatophore to the female. Drone honey-bees try to make sure that the virgin queen they have fertilized cannot easily mate again by leaving behind their genitalia as a mating plug. This suicidal behaviour prevents other males from forcibly mating with the queen, although she can remove the plug herself if she chooses. Once a queen has received sufficient sperm to fertilize all her eggs, she flies back to the hive with the evidence of her last conquest trailing from her abdomen. The male dies, but by preventing other males from mating the female against her will he increases the proportion of the eggs that his sperm will fertilize. A drone who could survive the ordeal would gain next to nothing. There is only one virgin queen for each colony, but a whole swarm of males, so a male that survived mating with one queen would be very unlikely to have a second opportunity. It is a better bet to try and make maximum use of his one stroke of luck than to try and mate again.

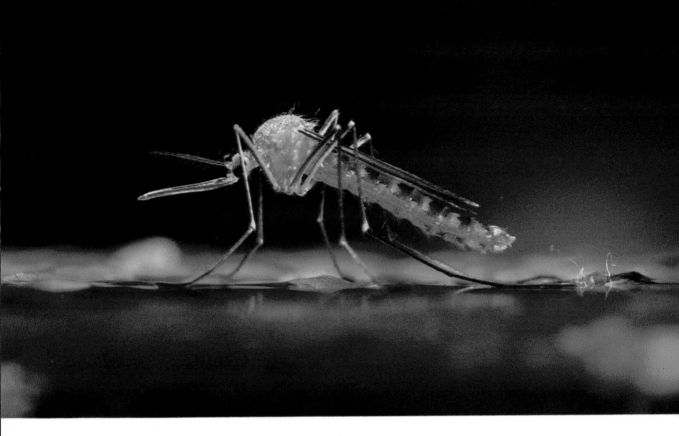

A newly emerged mosquito.

If the male is doomed to die in order to protect his investment in the young, why waste such a noble sacrifice? Male insectivorous midges never release themselves from the female after copulating. She eats her mate alive, leaving his genitalia as a plug to prevent other males from troubling her. Her mate, in effect, is supplying food for his young, a substantial contribution to their survival.

Plugs are also common among larger animals, although none are quite as dramatic in their insistence on chastity as the drone honey-bees or insectivorous midges. The mating plug which a male garter snake leaves in his mate contains a pheromone which makes her unattractive to the other males in the den, allowing her to escape further harassment. Mammals too sometimes produce a mating plug; guinea-pigs, hamsters, even chimpanzees produce a secretion from the prostate and which solidifies their semen, creating a physical barrier to the sperm of the next male and perhaps also preventing the backflow of semen from the uterus.

Plugs are not the only way of preventing other males from gaining access to females. Males of the small postman butterfly (*Heliconius erato*) make their mates unattractive to subsequent suitors by stuffing them full of a pheromone that makes them smell like males. Many butterflies can also produce enormous quantities of headless sperm which contain no genetic material and so can never fertilize an egg. These are easy to make, and with them the male fills the female's sperm storage sacs so that no other sperm can get in.

146

ABOVE *The male Apollo butterfly first loads up the female with headless sperm, so that there is no room in the female's sperm storage sacs for sperm from other males. He then secretes a special copulatory plug which temporarily seals the female's genital tract.*

RIGHT *Attempted takeover. A male dungfly tries to dislodge a successful male from the female that he is guarding.*

All these methods have one severe drawback. What if the female really would benefit from mating again? Females could evolve that are capable of removing the plugs or dissolving them, or of neutralizing the males' anti-aphrodisiac. Males too might develop pincers and tweezers to remove plugs from females if this would increase their reproductive success. These physical barriers do not guarantee protection, which is perhaps why male dungflies trust neither plugs nor offputting smells, but do the job themselves. Down among the grass with the cowpats as their stage, these beautiful yellow creatures act out a fascinating performance. Flies begin to arrive at a cowpat a few moments after it hits the ground, and on it they will mate and lay eggs. A female arriving at the pat is quickly jumped on by a male, who then begins fending off other males with his legs. Often they move into the grass nearby to escape the crush, but once they have mated, the female returns to the pat to lay her eggs, still carrying the male on her back. She stores his sperm in a sac which leads from her genital tract. The first sperm in is the last to get out, and if she mated again, the efforts of the first male would be almost entirely wasted. So although he could now leave and mate again, he stays with her, riding on her back to protect her from other males while she lays her eggs comparatively undisturbed. Once she has finished, she gives a little shake from side to side, the male dismounts and she makes a hasty departure.

Although the male dungfly stops copulating and simply defends the female while she lays, some male stick insects do not separate their genitalia, and remain locked together until the eggs are laid several weeks later. As a result a stick insect holds the record for the longest copulation ever recorded in the animal world – seventy-nine days.

Defending the female from gallivanting males is also important for some birds. Sand martins (or bank swallows, as they are called in the United States) are in many ways typical of monogamous birds. The male and female are difficult to tell apart, and both birds work together to build the nest, incubate the eggs, and feed the young once they have hatched. Nevertheless for a week after the pair has formed in spring the male guards the female, following her every time she leaves the nest. Sand martins nest in large colonies, since there are few suitable nesting sites, and above their sandbank scores of birds swoop and soar in aerobatic feeding flights. During the crucial period when the female is fertile, she is quickly joined by a group of males, perhaps able to guess at her condition by her heavy, laboured flight, but her mate stays close while she turns and weaves through the sky. Should she be separated from her mate, other males can sneak quick copulations which may fertilize some of the eggs, but once the female has laid her clutch the danger is over, and both the guarding by her mate and the chases by other males cease abruptly.

The mosquito with its waxy plug, the heliconid butterfly with his anti-aphrodisiac, and the dungflies and sand martins which guard their partners all enhance the contribution they make to the next generation by preventing other males from fertilizing their chosen

A sand martin leaves the nest carrying a fecal pellet from a young chick. Now the brood has hatched, male and female come and go independently, but earlier in the season the male jealously guards the female wherever she goes.

mates. But the male's investment must also be protected after the eggs have been fertilized, at least among lions, where the males have a macabre approach to improving their individual productivity. A male that successfully takes control of a pride begins his reign by killing off the cubs fathered by the previous male. Through this infanticide the new lion eliminates the possibility of later competition with his own cubs, and brings the females quickly back into estrus so that he can mate with them. Similar behaviour sometimes occurs when a new male takes over a troop of langur monkeys. In this case some of the young may survive, since the females are more able to protect their young, and often gang up against the male in response to his attacks.

chapter eight

The Female Fights Back

The stunning beauty of a male peacock displaying. To our eyes the male may seem to have the better deal once again, and we overlook the dusky females, as do their predators. The male's conspicuous and costly display is probably the result of females refusing to mate with all but the finest males.

Female Choice

In the battle of the sexes, the males have most of the weapons, and whenever they can avoid looking after the young they will use every possible means to try and fertilize more females. In the females' armoury there is often only one defence against the male onslaught, but its effect is devastating. Females can say no.

Males can fight for access to females and prevent them from mating with other males. The females accept most of these restraints. Males can bribe females by protecting a useful resource and allowing only their mates to use it. All this costs the female nothing. She too must mate to make sure of passing on her genes, and if the male can contribute nothing more than his genes to the young, what better mate could she choose than the one male capable of holding off the competition? The female that agrees to mate with a male honeyguide in order to be allowed to feed at his bees' nest may be succumbing to bribery, but when she refuses to mate with other males she is clearly making a choice. The males may appear to dominate the females, but it is ultimately the females that choose who they will mate with.

In the same way, the hind in a stag's harem has an easy time. She has no difficulty in choosing her mate since the fittest male in the area is by definition the one in charge of the harem (or the one capable of sneaking through his defences). Females are the prizes in the competition between the males, but they are at the same time the winners. Where males refuse to compete, females will sometimes encourage fights in order to help decide which is the more promising partner. Female mallards incite drakes to attack each other by performing a ritual display. The female swims towards her chosen partner, threatening another male over her shoulder. As she swims along, her neck is bent awkwardly and her feathers are flattened against her body as she quickly strokes her breast with her beak, her whole posture seeming to convey sheepish helplessness. The drake she has chosen must respond by attacking the nearest male, which he does by grabbing at the feathers of his crop and pushing backwards. Early in the mating season bare patches appear on the breasts of mallard drakes who have been the victims of the females' decision-making.

If no male is nearby to defend her, the female's response to pursuit by unwanted males is quite different. Instead of the ritualized sheepish display, she holds her head back on her shoulders and treatens with her beak open, making a sound quite different from her 'inciting' call.

Another case of females inciting males to violence has recently been reported in a small population of fiddler crabs on the coast of Panama. The males approach the females and hug them with their enlarged claws, directing them or carrying them to the burrows where they hope to mate. But the female is no pawn in this game. If she struggles, she can escape and this attracts more males to the area, who in turn try to lead her back to their own underground chambers. By protesting, the female improves her chances of finding a larger and presumably fitter male. Should she then decide that the burrow is unsuitable for her brood, she can still escape and select an alternative partner.

Even among elephant seals, where the top male seems to control everyone else, the female still retains a choice of sorts. She cannot resist being mated by the largest bull, who will be at least three times her weight and able to do as he pleases, but if she is mounted by a lesser bull she will protest violently, whipping her hind quarters from side to side and howling a train of vocal threats. If the top male is nearby, he will quickly drive away the interloper. However, even the most macho male can only look after a harem of forty or so females. He is kept busy, copulating continually day and night with only short breaks, and as the season wears on he may become an exhausted and unreliable mate. So although a female will benefit if the dominant male fertilizes her egg, she must also make absolutely sure that she is pregnant before leaving the beach, and towards the end of the breeding season a cow has nothing to loose and everything to gain by allowing other, inferior males to copulate. If she is already pregnant, the mating will do no harm, but if she has failed to conceive by the harem master, better to take a chance with an underling than risk a year without a pup. So as females move off to the sea, they are fair game for all and sundry and not a whimper of protest is heard.

How can biologists be sure that the female seals are really making a choice about whom they will mate with? The theory makes sense, but it is impossible to know for sure that a female seal is making a decision about her mate, even an unconscious, biologically programmed 'decision'. Perhaps females being mounted by the harem master do not protest because they are overawed by his size; perhaps towards the end of the season they are too weary to resist the mating attempts by subordinate males? Perhaps after all the dominant male really does

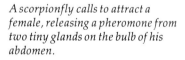

A scorpionfly calls to attract a female, releasing a pheromone from two tiny glands on the bulb of his abdomen.

have everything his own way. If we could find an animal where a single female willingly allowed dominant males to fertilize more of her eggs, and broke off copulation with inferior males of her own accord, the whole theory would be more credible. For such an example we must look away from the Antarctic and the world of the elephant seal to the temperate woodlands of the northern hemisphere.

Throughout the woodlands and hedgerows of Europe and North America, every large insect that dies becomes the focus of a minute frenzy of activity. The ubiquitous scavengers, ants and beetles, play their part in this, but the real vultures of the insect world are the scorpion-flies. Their long beaks tear into the corpses as they delve beneath the cuticle to get at the juicy flight muscles. A male does his best to keep the prize to himself, fending off newcomers with his tail claspers. Once he has gorged himself, the reason for his selfishness becomes clear. As dusk falls, he settles on a leaf and begins his courtship of the female that he had earlier driven from the carcase.

First he spreads his wings, lifts his abdomen, and exposes two small feathery glands near the tip. These release a pheromone which gently wafts through the woodland, drawing the female back to him. As she approaches, his activity increases: he flicks his abdomen up and down and vibrates his wings. There is now no trace of the violence he exhibited earlier. Instead he starts his mouth-parts working and produces a drop of spittle, which he gently passes to her. As she feeds on it, he clasps her abdomen and they begin to copulate. The larger his spittle ball, the longer the female will feed, and the longer she feeds, the more eggs he can fertilize. A small ball that keeps the female going for a mere five minutes gives the male time to transfer only a few hundred sperm; more spittle, offered repeatedly, will keep the female happy for an hour or more. As soon as his gifts of food run out, she runs out on him too.

Because the female can end the copulation whenever it suits her, the pressure is very much on the male to find food and make spittle balls. With competition from other males and from the scavenging ants and beetles, food is often scarce, and the males must resort to raiding spiders' webs for their dead insects, a risky business which often results in the scorpionflies themselves becoming a meal. Desperate males may grab at females and try to mate them by force, but this approach is rarely successful, as the female can usually struggle free.

It is just this sort of pressure on the male which encourages the evolution of sneaky male tactics, and in North America the hanging-fly, a close relative of the scorpionfly, has come up with one remarkable trick. Like the scorpionfly, the male hanging-flies must also present their partners with food offerings, either a spittle ball or a dead insect, and if times are hard they too will raid spiders' webs. There is, however, another, much easier way to get hold of a present for the intended partner. A male that sees another signalling with a nuptial gift clasped in his legs will alight beside him and lower his wings, imitating the stylized behaviour usually only performed by females. If the transvestite male can keep his abdomen away from the searching

Mating scorpionflies. The female (on the right) is feeding on a small spittle ball, which she holds in her jaws.

claspers of the signalling male for long enough to get a firm grip on the dead insect he is being offered, he will make off with the prize and begin courting on his own account. The strategy is a lot less dangerous than crawling about in spiders' webs, but like the scorpionfly's attempt to mate by force, it is not often successful, and the males of both species are thus driven at times to risk their lives. When males are driven to such desperate measures, it demonstrates how much pressure the females can apply by choosing their mates.

Displays of Prowess

In the animal world, there are the flashy here-today, gone-tomorrow males that do nothing to look after their young, and the solid dependable types who will share in the work. In deciding whom to mate with, a female would do well to consider the role that her male must play. Fly-by-night males that will not help with the brood can only be selected on the rather dubious evidence of how good their genes appear to be, but males who will be expected to perform parental tasks like feeding the young can be put through a much more rigorous and practical examination. Courtship feeding is one realistic test and it is common among birds.

The bee-eater provides a good example of an animal where the male is put through his paces. Bee-eaters remain paired throughout the breeding season and the male will help the female to excavate the nest hole and to feed the young. But courtship feeding among European bee-eaters begins immediately the birds arrive from their African wintering grounds. While the female watches nearby, the male catches a large insect, and returns to perch beside her, fanning his tail and calling loudly. She usually accepts the insect from him and then lies almost horizontally across the branch with her feathers ruffled, while the male copulates. Everything can be over so quickly that the female is still trying to swallow her gift as the male dismounts.

A male red-throated bee-eater (Merops bullocki) presents an insect to his mate. Courtship feeding is common in birds, and in bee-eaters is often followed immediately by copulation.

Courtship feeding by the male bee-eater may continue until all the eggs have been laid, and is probably vital in keeping the pair together as well as being an important contribution to the female's diet. Among common terns the nutritional importance of courtship feeding is clear. The more food the male brings, the more eggs the female lays, and females judge males on the number of fish that they provide early in the season. At first the male is reluctant to give up his fish and just flies around the colony showing them to females, but as a relationship develops, the males feed the females more and more readily. For red-billed gulls, the breeding season is shorter and females are already committed to a male before courtship feeding starts, so a female cannot select her mate on the basis of his feeding performance, but she will refuse to pair again with a male that failed to keep her well supplied during the previous season.

By selecting a male who can prove himself worthy by bringing home the fish, the female benefits in two ways. Although the male's genes may be no better than average, she at least makes certain that there is nothing seriously wrong with him, and so she selects a suitable genetic father for her young. She also receives more food to help her produce those young. Although it is common among birds, courtship feeding is not the only criterion on which females judge their mates' likely performance as fathers. Some animals select their mates simply on the evidence of their size and aggression, since large mates will often be better at defending the young. The female stickleback prefers to mate with males who already have eggs in their nest. As the nest fills up the male spends more time protecting the eggs and less time chasing after females, so the last eggs to be laid in a nest are the best protected.

A male roseate tern presents his mate with a fish.

RIGHT Immature bald eagles practise for the day when their flying skills will have to impress a potential mate.

The female spring peeper, a North American tree-frog, selects males whose calls are faster and deeper than their rivals. This may seem an arbitrary way to select a partner, but it is actually very sensible. Males that call more frequently are more likely to insert a call into a brief moment of silence in the cacophony and this will help the females to find them. Deeper croaks are made by larger males; since frogs grow throughout their lives, larger males are generally older males, so a deep croak certifies that a male has been able to cope with his environment, to grow and prosper. His genes are those of a survivor, and a female could certainly do worse than mate with a male who has proved himself capable of finding food and avoiding predators.

Male eagles and other birds of prey demonstrate their suitability as mates in other ways; they put on spectacular aerobatic displays. On his return to the breeding grounds towards the end of February, the male hen-harrier shows off his skills to his intended mate in an awesome display of flying ability. He climbs steeply for 30 metres (100 ft) or more, then rolls or somersaults before plummeting recklessly earthward. Just as it seems that he has misjudged his dive and must inevitably crash head-first into the ground, he pulls up and begins to climb once more, repeating the performance over and over again. While it is not certain that this display helps females to choose between males, it is clear enough that its main function is not to attract a mate. The display begins only after a female has arrived in the area, and is seen much more frequently when several birds are nesting close together, and there is rivalry between the males. Soon after a display, a suitably impressed female will join the male to inspect the proposed nest site, secure in the knowledge that her intended partner can at least fly like a harrier should.

Displays of Artistry

One look at a peacock should be enough to convince anyone that Darwin's theory of natural selection is nonsense. Nothing so gaudy, bright and bizarre could possibly be the result of the simple process of chance mutation and the survival of the fittest. Can we really be expected to believe that the peacock, struggling under the burden of its impossible tail, is better equipped to survive life in a tropical rainforest than ordinary birds?

Darwin, of course, expected no such thing, although he was well aware that he had a good deal of explaining to do before he could even begin to persuade his critics that these psychedelic displays could find a place in his essentially utilitarian theory. About the display of the closely related argus pheasant, he wrote:

> He who thinks he can safely gauge the discrimination and taste of the lower animals, may deny that the female argus pheasant can appreciate such refined beauty; but he will then be compelled to admit that the extraordinary attitudes assumed by the male during the act of courtship, by which the wonderful beauty of the plumage is fully displayed, are purposeless; and this is a conclusion which I for one will never admit.

By 'extraordinary attitudes', Darwin meant the way in which the argus pheasant spreads his wings in a fan shape, displaying a set of eyes very like those of the peacock's tail. The problem of explaining how Nature could possibly have selected such dramatic forms is the same in both cases.

Although the spotted wings of the argus pheasant might conceivably be good camouflage in the dappled light of its forest home, it is pushing credulity beyond its limits to suggest that this is the only function of the peacock's tail, or for that matter that the enormous size of the tail helps the bird to fly through the trees, although both theories have had their proponents. Because the full beauty and splendour of the peacock's tail are only revealed when the male is courting a female, it seems most likely that the glorious and regular patterning have something to do with encouraging her to mate with him. Exactly how his tail does this is still, as it always has been, a matter of controversy.

Most theories assume that the display somehow allows females to select the fittest male. When he will contribute nothing but his genes to the offspring, females might be expected to choose between males on the evidence of how good these genes might be, and if elaborate displays could somehow convey information about a male's genes, then this would help the female to make an appropriate choice. One interesting theory is that the male is actually showing off his handicap, as if boasting that he is so fit that he can survive despite his

A superb lyre bird (Menura novaehollandae) shows off his tail.

European wrens are polygamous, and have intricately woven songs. The songs of their monogamous relatives are less complicated.

enormous burden. But the theory has a weakness, for while a female might secure better genes for her young by mating with a handicapped bird, the chicks would also inherit the burden and in the end would be no better off.

Another possibility is that males with brightly coloured plumage are showing off their rude physical health, their freedom from the parasites that might make their feathers dull and dowdy. This idea has rather more support, for polygamous and brightly coloured birds do indeed seem to suffer from more parasitic infestations. If females begin choosing brightly coloured males as mates, then selection might favour those males with the brightest plumage, leading to the vivid and intense colours that are so common in these species where one male mates with many females. Once females are programmed to mate with the gaudiest males, the scene is set for the evolution of the peacock's tail. From each new generation, the females select only the brightest, most outrageous males. It no longer matters that the bright colours expose the males to predators, or that the longer feathers make moving about in the forest more and more difficult. Any male that cannot perform the display will not mate, however long he lives. Even if a display of health was the original message, males with long and gaudy tails may now be lying through their feathers about their physical state, since it seems that in this system there is nothing much to prevent them from cheating. Males could well have evolved so that if they became infected or diseased, then the last place that they showed it was their courtship behaviour. However, keeping his train preened and glossy may well take the peacock so long that it really is an honest indicator of the animal's state of health and his efficiency at his other tasks. Only when the sheer size and weight of their tails becomes such a cumbersome burden that the owners are likely to be killed before mating, will selection call a halt to the process.

Whatever the reason, we can only assume that the female chooses between males on the evidence of their courtship performance, and that once the females begin to select males with extravagant plumage, there is nothing to prevent the evolution of the shamelessly ostentatious peacock's tail. The gaudy skirts and fans and the iridescent capes of many birds of paradise are similar evolutionary creations that are difficult to explain in any other way. So too are the extremely complex songs of the wren, the sedge warbler and the mocking bird.

Complex songs, like elaborate plumage, are the sign of considerable sexual competition between males. Polygamous wrens have more elaborate songs than closely related monogamous species that form permanent pairs, and presumably the male with the most intricate song, like the peacock with the prettiest tail, gets the most opportunities to mate. Monogamous males will also compete for females when, as often happens, the first pairs to breed can raise the largest families. The extraordinary sequence of trills and whistles that makes up the liquid song of the sedge warbler is a serenade intended to attract females, and although the male will mate only once, the larger his vocal repertoire, the sooner he will attract a mate and the more successfully he will breed.

The complex song of the sedge warbler, the bright plumage of many male birds and the courtship livery of many fishes can make the males conspicuous and a target for predators. Many animals minimize the dangers by shedding their courtship dress as soon as the breeding season is over and taking on a more sombre and better-camouflaged appearance, but male bower birds seem to have avoided the problem altogether. Although close relatives of the birds of paradise, bower birds are generally rather frumpish creatures that attract little attention to themselves. Instead of carrying their sexual advertisements around in their plumage, bower birds persuade females to mate by displaying neither their bodies nor carefully woven songs, but by creating a new art form. The 'bower' which gives the bird its name can take many forms. The stagemaker bower bird from Northern Australia clears every piece of rubbish from an area one or two metres across and then decorates it with a large number of green leaves, which he places carefully upside down on his display ground. The great grey bower bird builds a narrow avenue of sticks, twigs and grass stems, which he decorates in front and behind with stones, wallaby bones, shells, fruits, leaves, glass and bits of metal, showing again a preference for green objects. The satin bower bird prefers blue, and builds a similar structure of twigs, decorated with blue flowers and bluish feathers. As if this were not enough to impress the female, the satin bower bird also paints the walls of his bower with a paste made from charcoal dust and saliva which he rubs over the twigs with the side of his beak.

LEFT *The drab fawn-breasted bower bird tries to impress a female with his choice of decoration and his remarkable architectural skill.*

OPPOSITE *The related great bird of paradise instead uses his plumage to attract attention.*

BELOW LEFT *Male magnificent frigate birds help their mates raise the young for a time, but then desert them and begin trying to form a new pair. Consequently there is stiff competition between males for access to the few available females, and the males have evolved this elaborate display.*

BELOW RIGHT *Folded-wing fireflies displaying. In this species, the males sit in trees and flash in unison.*

While the inconspicuous bower birds have adopted sophisticated methods of attracting mates and avoiding predators, other animals may keep out of trouble by displaying in groups; with many eyes to watch for predators, animals distracted by courtship are less likely to meet an untimely end. Often, as with the common grey tree-frog (*Hyla versicolor*), the males defend tiny territories (in this case by head-butting other males, kicking at them with their hind legs, or simply jumping on them). A female is then attracted to the call of a particular male, hops up to him and mates. Male hammer-headed bats set up small territories at traditional sites in their African rainforest home, and then simply sit around in trees and attract females by honking at them. The hammer-headed bat is one of the ugliest African mammals, at least by the esthetic standards of most humans, with a grotesquely swollen mouth and nose. Yet somehow the female chooses a male to

mate with, settles beside him and quickly copulates. Even insects have similar male-group displays, and the folded-wing fireflies from the mangrove swamps of Thailand provide a spectacular example. Here thousands, even millions of fireflies display in synchrony, lighting up whole river banks with their flashing signals like a long line of Christmas trees.

When this sort of display was first studied, it was assumed that by congregating in groups the males were working together to increase the impact of their advertising and to attract females from a wider area with their more impressive performance. This theory seemed a particularly plausible explanation for the massed choruses of cicadas, crickets and frogs, which can sometimes be deafening to human ears. Although the increased volume makes the calls audible slightly further away, there are more males making them, and all the evidence suggests that while the louder calling and more conspicuous visual displays do indeed attract more females, the number of females to each male stays almost exactly the same.

More recently it has been suggested that these group displays are necessary to arouse the female who has evolved resistance to courtship by single males and is only turned on by the stimulation of a large group. A female being courted by several males can make a well-judged choice about whom she mates with, although quite how females choose between different males in these gatherings (usually called 'leks' from the Swedish for 'play') is yet another mystery. Sometimes it seems that females prefer a particular territory and so for instance among prairie chickens it is the males who hold central territories in the lek that get the most offers, but in other animals, success is unconnected with a male's position. The male white-bearded manakin defends the same miniature territory throughout his life. This small forest bird from the Caribbean clears a patch on the ground where he will perform a display of acrobatics to any female who comes to visit. Accompanied by mechanical cracks and grunts, made by twisting his feathers as he flaps his wings, he prances about, competing for attention with the twenty or so other males in the same display area.

Even among apparent equals on a lek there may be subtle differences. So with the synchronously flashing fireflies there is some evidence that the 'chorus leader', the male who flashes slightly ahead of the others, is likely to be the females' favourite. Among some toads, the male with the deepest croak attracts most females, a clever move on the female's part since these males are likely to be bigger, and bigger of course means better at finding food. Since toads grow throughout their lives, bigger generally also means older, and a male that has lived long enough to make a deep croak must also have been good at avoiding his enemies. From the pitch of a male's call, the female gains a great deal of useful information.

Whatever feature it is that the female is using to make her choice, the group displays make it easier for her to compare prospective partners, and the result is that only a few males at the lek succeed in mating. In

Blackcocks (Lyrarus tetrix) displaying at a lek.

Three female ruffs watch a male prostrate himself in an attempt to persuade them to mate with him. Ruffs display in groups and competition between males is fierce. White-collared males never become dominant in these gatherings, but adopt an alternative lifestyle as peripheral or satellite males. They may be important in establishing new display areas.

one study of North American prairie chickens, the two dominant males in a group of about twenty birds were responsible for over eighty per cent of all the matings observed. This sort of intense competition puts pressure on the males, and males that cannot compete according to the rules come up with alternative ways of persuading females to mate. Peripheral males may chase after females at the edge of the lek, or intercept them as they move towards the centre. Often the peripheral males are young birds whose chances to dominate the lek will not come for some years, but the unaggressive white-collared ruffs that are driven from the lek by dominant dark-headed birds will live their entire lives as satellite males.

In leking birds, as in polygamous species generally, the males are bigger and often brightly coloured with bizarre and striking plumage. It is these gaudy show-offs who are the stars of the natural world; in zoos, visitors gaze at them in awe and overlook the camouflaged, skulking females in the same enclosure. However, it is for these females that the glorious princes of the animal kingdom put on their performance. By exercising their choice, the females are manipulating the entire show; they are the power behind the throne.

Damselflies

Perhaps the lesson of this and the preceding chapter is that the battle of the sexes can never be won. It is an endless war of attrition, both sides struggling to gain the upper hand, but restrained by their ultimate dependence on each other. Males compete to fertilize as many females as possible, and females struggle to get the best deal they can. Biologists are beginning to learn that whenever one sex appears to be winning the battle, the other is probably doing something very devious that they have completely overlooked. By separating the male and female views of the struggle, we have tried to show how the demands of each sex differ, but it would be misleading to leave this fascinating sexual conflict altogether without putting the two sexes back together again and seeing how they get on. We would expect males to fight, to prevent other males from mating, or to protect their mates, and we would expect females to exploit this sexual competition between the males whenever they can. As we shall see, damselflies do all this and more.

Damselflies are the large and brightly coloured insects that must be familiar to anyone who has picnicked beside a pond or river on a summer's day. In the common brown damselfly (*Calopteryx maculata*) from North America, the males are territorial, perching on a reed or twig. With their tail up and wings open, they threaten other males, attacking any that fly too close. To be worth defending, their territory must contain at least one suitable egg-laying site, which the male uses as a bribe in order to persuade the female to mate. When a female damselfly approaches, the resident male stays on his perch and displays by lifting his abdomen and lowering his back wings, which are otherwise held closed above his back. If the female lands, he courts her by hovering in front of her, and if she does not fly away, he attempts to land on her back and grasp her with the claspers at the end of his abdomen. This puts his genital opening immediately above her head, where she cannot possibly reach it, and so at the same time he smears sperm on to a special copulatory organ beneath his belly. He then lifts the female, who can now bring her abdomen forward beneath her to complete the mating ring and collect the sperm from the male. Before passing his sperm, the male inserts his peculiarly shaped copulatory organ and cleans out the female's genital tract with a hook-shaped tool that empties her of sperm from previous matings. Copulation lasts for a minute or so, and for most of this time the male can be seen gently rocking up and down as he scrapes away, removing the sperm from the female. Only in the last few seconds is his own sperm transferred. From the male's point of view, if the female is gong to lay her eggs on his territory, it is only fair that the young should be fathered by him and not by some other male.

At this point it seems that the male is running the show. A pair of damselflies is more vulnerable to predation than a lone insect and the female, perhaps still laden with sperm from a previous mating, appears to be risking her life just so that the male will let her lay eggs in

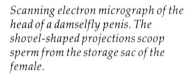

Scanning electron micrograph of the head of a damselfly penis. The shovel-shaped projections scoop sperm from the storage sac of the female.

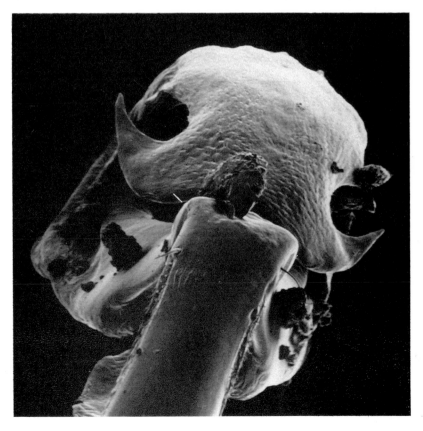

169

his territory. What is worse, she must first suffer the indignity of being cleansed by the male. But things are not quite so simple.

If female damselflies really did suffer through this treatment then, once fertilized, they would do better to lay their eggs when the males were less active, or in quiet corners of the pond where there were suitable egg-laying sites but no perches for the male to sit on and control territory. Instead, females almost always lay when there are males around. With a sharp egg-laying tool at the tip of her abdomen, a female cuts tiny holes into the stems of aquatic plants to push in a single egg, working her way along a length of stem near the water surface. In bad weather, she may be dragged under by the movement of the plants, or swamped by miniature waves, and for a waterlogged female it is a struggle to escape. Since the female is already loaded with his sperm, the father is chiefly interested in keeping other males away from her, but fortunately for the female, other males are only too pleased to perform an air-sea rescue mission and lift her clear, if they can. The female does not always copulate with the male that saves her, but the success rate for the males must be high enough for rescuing drowning damsels to be a worthwhile strategy to pursue. This success rate is much increased by the new male's ability to remove her previous mate's sperm and to fertilize the next batch of eggs himself.

Exactly why the female lets him do this is still a puzzle for biologists Presumably a female could evolve whose sperm storage sacs were out of reach of the male's scraper. She could then take advantage of the male's enthusiasm to rescue her without accepting him as a mate. Perhaps if she refused to form a mating wheel, the male would simply refuse to let her go, and so her chances of being snapped up by a predator would be even greater if she did not cooperate. Perhaps the female actually benefits through being cleaned out by the males who rescue her, since unlike her first mate, her subsequent mates must first prove themselves capable of lifting her out of the water. It is even possible that if all the females were to make their sperm sacs inaccessible to males, the males would simply stop bothering to rescue drowning females. As a result the species as a whole might be eliminated through competition with other damselfly species on the same lake. On the other hand, the evolution of 'cheating' females might encourage the appearance of females who could signal their willingness to be cleaned out by a male. The war of attrition between males and females looks like being a promising arena for students of biology for many years to come.

Damselflies mating.

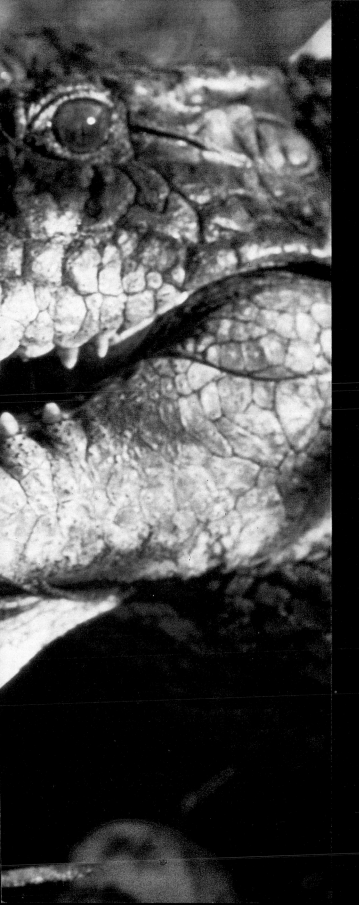

chapter nine

Parenthood

A female Nile crocodile carries her brood in her mouth. She lays her eggs in a hole on the riverbank and covers them with sand. Then she guards the nest night and day for three months or more, never leaving it even to feed. When the young eventually hatch, she digs them out, helping any that cannot rupture their shells themselves by gently cracking the eggs between her fearsome jaws. Although such a display of parental tenderness is surprising from an animal that we normally think of as sinister and dangerous, the female crocodile conforms to the stereotype of the caring mother. The father takes no part in looking after the young. Why then do most male birds help raise their broods, while many male fishes, frogs and insects take complete responsibility for looking after the young?

Life, Sex and the Problems of Parents

As human beings, we inevitably have a biased opinion of what it means to be a parent, for we devote more time to caring for our offspring than any other creature on the planet. By giving this sort of concentrated help to our children, we try to guarantee that they will survive to reproduce themselves, but children are so demanding that women can bear and raise only a few. By contrast, animals, like the oviparous oyster, that take no care of their offspring (see 'Breeding Seasons') lay fifteen to 115 million eggs at each spawning and will spawn several times during the summer. Many of these eggs will never be fertilized, and even for those eggs that hatch into larvae, several perilous weeks of drifting in the sea lie ahead. Of those that make it to the end of their journey, only a few larvae will settle where they can develop into young oysters.

This all adds up to a hazardous beginning for baby oysters, but it does not mean that oysters would be better off if they adopted the human approach to parenting. Unless the larval oyster lands somewhere with a firm anchorage and enough room to develop, it is doomed. Stuck to a rock, the parents can do little to help, except to produce as many embryos as possible. Weeds that invade disturbed ground, or plants that colonize woodland glades share the oyster's problem. They are immobile, and their patch will disappear as soon as the surrounding vegetation establishes itself. The best seed-bed for their offspring may be many miles away in any direction and all they can do is produce thousands of seeds and hope for the best. In one year only a few seedlings will establish themselves, but when a tree falls or a field is ploughed thousands of seeds may germinate and grow. Sowthistle (*Sonchus oleraceus*) can produce 25,000 seeds a year and red goosefoot (*Chenopodium rubrum*) can produce 176,000 seeds a year. Because they grow quickly and invest little energy in protecting the seeds, small plants like shepherd's purse (*Capsella bursa-pastoris*) may produce several generations in a single season, giving a parent plant the theoretical possibility of 64,000 million offspring a year from its relatively poor crop of 4,000 seeds from each generation. This is not the record, however, which is held by the giant puffball whose annual production of spores is upwards of seven million million for every fruiting body.

Careless parents, whether oysters or weeds, are capable of sudden and dramatic population explosions if conditions are right, but the more protection a plant or animal provides for its eggs, the fewer offspring it can produce. The double coconut, a native of the Seychelles, produces no more than eleven fruits at a time and each takes ten years to grow to its full size of about 20 kilogrammes (44 lb). So massive is the investment by the parent plant that the trees cannot even begin to bear fruit until they are thirty years old and well established. Instead of ensuring success by setting thousands of seeds which might produce a bumper crop in a good year, the double coconut has a different strategy. It provides a massive food supply for the young seedling and protects it with a tough shell from predators, helping each individual plant to get a good start and to elbow its way into the competitive jungle. Protection and a good start in life are essential if its seedlings are to survive in a stable, complex community where specialist seed-eaters abound and competition is intense.

Just as varied are the ways of life open to animals. At one extreme is the oyster with her millions of eggs and at the other the Californian condors. These are massive birds of prey that raise a single chick every two years and invest so much energy and effort in each breeding attempt that afterwards the parents must take a year off to recover. Between these two extremes lie many shades of compromise. Animals which release their eggs and sperm to be fertilized independently of the parents must produce very large numbers of each in order to ensure at least some success. To cut down on the number of eggs they must produce, most animals move closer to each other, concentrating the eggs and sperm into a smaller space and so improving the chances that the eggs will be fertilized.

Pairing has made it possible for animals that fertilize their eggs externally to adopt some very sophisticated tricks for concentrating their eggs and sperm, and so allows them to reduce the number of eggs, increase their size and provide specialized protection. Some of the most interesting examples are provided by fishes. The bitterling is a small freshwater fish from eastern Europe. In the breeding season, the female develops a long egg-laying tube, the tip of which reaches well past her tail fin. She uses this to introduce her eggs down the exhalant spout of a freshwater mussel. To stop the mussel from closing its shell while she is egg laying, she nudges it first with her mouth until it has become accustomed to the disturbance. Then as she lays her eggs, the male swims nearby and releases his sperm. This is drawn in through the mussel's inhalant siphon and fertilization takes place in the gills of the unwitting host. Inside the mussel's protective shell, the eggs develop for about a month, until the young can swim freely and avoid at least some of their enemies.

Another group of fishes, the mouthbrooders, adopt a very different but no less elegant approach. The female of the African mouthbrooding fish *Haplochromis wingatii* lays her eggs at the bottom of her pond. As she does so, the male swims about releasing his milt, but almost before he has begun, the female snatches the eggs into her mouth. At this stage the eggs are well protected from predators, but probably not fertilized. The female then attempts to take a row of eggs from the anal fin of the male. These eggs are actually only markings on the fin, but they look sufficiently like haplochromis' eggs to encourage the female, and set against the dark background of the fin they are very conspicuous. The male's milt is still being released from behind the anal fin, and as the female tries to pick up the egg-markings, she sucks in a mouthful of sperm, ensuring the fertilization of the eggs she is already holding. Other mouthbrooding fishes have evolved other methods for making certain that the eggs they protect so carefully have been fertilized. In Lake Mweru, on the border between Zaire and Zambia,

OPPOSITE *Weighing 20 kilograms (44 lb), the fruit of the Seychelles double coconut is the largest on earth, but the tree can only produce ten a year.* RIGHT *By contrast, the puffball releases millions of minute spores.*

ABOVE Many cichlid fishes protect their eggs by carrying them around in their mouths, and do not eat until they hatch. The young fry continue to return to the safety of their mother's mouth when danger threatens.

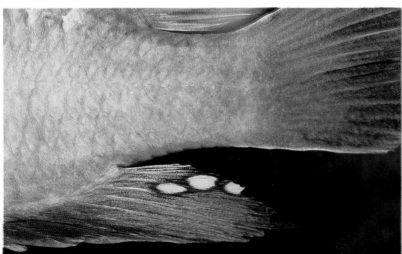

LEFT Egg dummies on the anal fin of a cichlid fish.

lives *Tilapia macrochir*. In the breeding season a conspicuous genital tassel hangs from the vent of the male, long filaments of tissue festooned with white, egg-like blobs which again are used to encourage the female to take a mouthful of the male's sperm.

The grunion, *Leuresthes tenuis*, is a little fragile fish found in a small area of shallow water off the coast of California, and like the mouth-brooding fishes it ensures that its eggs are fertilized and provides protection for the offspring at the same time, in this case by laying them in the shallow surf high on a beach. When the moon is full and the tide is at its highest, the female, accompanied by at least one male, swims into the shallow surf at the edge of the water and burrowing into the sand with her tail she makes a small, shallow pit. Lying alongside her, the male releases his milt into the sand where she buries her eggs. Often a group will be stranded on the beach until another wave reaches high enough to wash them back into the sea. Concentrated into such a small space with the sperm, the eggs can hardly fail to be fertilized; but the grunion does more than ensure the

successful meeting of its gametes. Like the mouthbrooding fishes, it is also providing protection for its offspring. Spring tides occur twice every month, when the moon is full and again two weeks later when it is new. For two weeks the eggs of the grunion lie buried in the damp sand, out of the way of any fish that might make a tasty snack of them. Not until the next spring tide two weeks later will the waves once more break across the sand. Only then do the eggs hatch and the larvae swim off into the sea.

Animals like the grunion and the mouthbrooding fishes, which do more for their young than simply release a batch of tiny eggs and sperm into the sea, must compromise by producing fewer eggs than their careless competitors. The grunion must store her eggs until the full moon when conditions are exactly right for their release. Constantly to carry a full load of ripe eggs would be a serious burden for the female fish. However, by providing the young with protection she improves their chances of making it into the next generation in the competitive, predator-ridden ocean.

Animals which fertilize their eggs inside the body of the female take this protection an important step further. Brooding starfishes, sea urchins, sponges and the edible oyster all draw in sperm with the water that aerates their bodies allowing the eggs to be fertilized. So the embryos develop and grow without leaving the protection of the mother. On land, reptiles, birds and mammals carry their eggs around at least briefly before laying or giving birth. Such animals need not adopt the subtle tricks to protect the offspring which are used by parents whose eggs are fertilized externally. Although the young of internally fertilized animals are already protected and are usually large and well developed when they emerge into the world, they are

A beadlet anemone ejects one of the young that it has been brooding.

often entirely dependent on at least one of their parents. Among mammals it is generally the mother, among insects often the father, and in birds it is usually both parents who end up with the responsibility of looking after the young. As we shall see, sex also has a part to play in deciding who is left holding the baby.

Monogamy

For most of the natural world, polygamy is the rule and monogamy the rare exception. Less than three per cent of all mammals are monogamous, even fewer fishes, and in most other groups monogamy is almost unheard of. The exceptions are the birds, of which over ninety per cent have only one mate at a time.

Birds are unusual in many ways. The power of flight allows them to search enormous areas for their food, but it also requires a large amount of energy. To support their frantic flapping, small humming-birds must drink twice their body-weight of nectar every day, and even the more leisurely songbirds need a daily supply of up to a third of their weight in food. To meet these needs and still have some energy left over to raise a brood of hungry chicks is a demanding task. The growing young need food themselves and they also need to be kept warm and protected from danger.

Male birds can perform all these tasks. They can build the nest, brood the eggs, collect food and scare off predators. Very few male animals find themselves able to contribute as much to their offspring. A newborn foal or lamb is on its feet in hours and is fed exclusively by its mother. The only contribution that its father can make is to look threatening whenever trouble looms. He cannot even help provide food for his mate as can dog-foxes and other hunting animals. If the stallion or ram can do nothing to help its young once they are born, the best way to ensure a thriving family is to go out and mate again as quickly as possible.

Birds like the wandering albatross and the condor which will exhaust themselves raising a single chick every two years could not breed at all if the male deserted the female immediately the eggs were laid. For most pairs, there is a conflict of interest between the sexes. If the female can raise some of the brood alone, a male would probably father more young by being promiscuous, but the female would raise more offspring by forcing the male to stay with her and help raise the brood. Many monogamous birds have long periods of courtship, sometimes 'keeping company' for several seasons before beginning to breed, and it has been suggested that this extended courtship helps females to find out whether or not the male is being faithful, or is stimultaneously trying to form a pair with another bird.

Some birds (geese, swans, albatrosses and kittiwakes to name only a few) remain faithful not just for a season, but for life. This saves the birds the trouble of finding a new mate every season, which may be particularly important for birds breeding in high latitudes where the

OPPOSITE *A male kingfisher brings food to the nest. In many bird species, males can raise more young by cooperating with females to raise the brood than by deserting their partners and attempting to mate again.*

season is short. Pinkfooted geese (*Anser brachyrhynchus*) arriving in Iceland in mid-May from their wintering grounds in Britain have until the end of August to mate, build their nests, lay their eggs and raise young that are strong enough to fly south and escape the coming Arctic winter. In early May, the nest site is still covered with snow and in mid-August the marshy ground begins to freeze again, quickly killing off the tender green shoots on which the birds feed. In seasons when the snow lies late in spring, the geese may not be able to breed at all. Every day counts and by being 'married' on arrival in Iceland, the birds need waste no time with finding a mate and courting. Some birds will already have mated before flying north, so that almost as soon as their rudimentary nest is built, the female is ready to lay. With such a tight schedule, this could mean the difference between successfully raising four youngsters and failing to breed at all.

Birds which breed in more temperate latitudes and at a more leisurely pace must gain rather different benefits from lifelong marriage. Kittiwakes whose eggs are destroyed by predators may have time to lay again in the same season, a luxury impossible for the pinkfoot, and yet like the pinkfoot, kittiwakes mate for life. For the kittiwakes there is less urgency, but mating for life still allows married pairs to begin breeding earlier. The first pairs to lay each year raise more young on average, and there are other advantages too. Their experience of each other helps them to cooperate more effectively in caring for their young, and birds that have bred together in previous seasons often lay larger eggs and more of them. Experienced pairs usually get the best nesting sites, the ones nearest to the centre of the colony and best protected from predators.

Lifelong 'marriage' is an advantage for kittiwakes, but not essential. If a pair fails to breed successfully in one year, the partners will probably 'divorce', and the next year each will try again with a new partner. Their marriage is a pragmatic affair, not an emotional involvement that somehow transcends their biological needs. Among pinkfooted geese divorce rates are very low indeed, but this is a reflection of their more demanding breeding strategy, not an indication that geese are more moral birds.

While 'marriage' is characteristic of birds, some other animals are also monogamous. Gibbons and siamangs form life-long partnerships, the only apes which always do so. A pair of Kloss's gibbons will produce young every other year and live together with their sub-adult offspring as a family group. When the young reach maturity, at about eight years old, the parents will help them to establish their own territory. Territorial competition between gibbons is intense, and an orphaned sub-adult male has little chance of establishing himself in a vacant patch against competition from other young males that are supported by their parents. If a male's family line is to be continued, he must stay with the family group and provide support for his young in these territorial take-overs.

As with many birds, there are male mammals that can raise more offspring by staying with a single female than by deserting the mother

and her young to try their luck elsewhere. Nest building by males is rare in mammals, but beavers are monogamous and the male co-operates with the female in building their dam, their lodge, and in collecting the enormous quantities of food needed in order to survive the winter. In monkeys, monogamy is more common when the young at birth are large relative to the size of the mother. The male marmoset begins to carry the young immediately they are born, while in tamarins, where the young are smaller, the male often does not begin carrying them for several days or even weeks.

Most monogamous animals maintain their bond to each other through aggression towards intruders. Sometimes the male alone is responsible, jealously guarding his territory and keeping out all other animals of the same species. Occasionally, as with the beaver, it is the female who takes the active role. In many animals, aggression is primarily between members of the same sex, the male chasing off other males and the female dealing with intrusive females. This is clearly the case in the blind goby, a small fish that spends almost its entire life hiding in a burrow at the bottom of a rock pool. The burrow is usually occupied by a single pair, and although the fish cannot see, each recognizes other individuals of the same sex by their smell and drives them away.

A pair of pinkfooted geese on the way to a successful breeding season.

Siamangs will remain together as a family until the juvenile is ready to set up on its own.

RIGHT Spider monkeys are polygamous. The young are small at birth and easily carried by the mother without help from the father.

Young albatrosses 'keep company'
for several seasons before beginning
to breed, and continually perform
their courtship displays throughout
the breeding season. These dances
may help strengthen the bond
between the parents.

Role Reversal

In their struggle against male chauvinism, female animals almost always hold their own. Their ability to choose between males counterbalances the smaller physiological contribution that males make to their young. In exceptional circumstances, the female may even find herself in a position to dominate the male. Natural selection will usually favour the errant male who leaves his female looking after the young and searches for a new mate; but if fertilization is external, the female can often escape while the male is still busy fertilizing the eggs. The male is literally left holding the babies, and he must decide whether to stay and look after them or just leave them to their own devices.

Many factors will influence the male's decision. What are the chances that the young will survive if he deserts them, and how much better are their chances if he stays? If the eggs are well concealed, or protected in some other way, the male might as well leave them even if there is little chance of him finding another mate. On the other hand if the eggs are considered haute cuisine by the local predators and could benefit from the male's attention, then he is unlikely to desert them.

If he eventually stays, he will perhaps be putting more energy into raising the young than the female, and once this happens it is the male who becomes choosey about whom he will mate with, and the females who compete for the opportunity to mate. Sometimes the traditional roles are reversed, since the males' parenting duties make them a scarce commodity, and in response females often initiate and play an active role in courtship, since it is they who must now persuade the coy males to mate. There is no sharp divide between maternal and paternal care, but rather a gentle gradation from those species in which the male contributes only his sperm to the young, through animals where both parents contribute equally to raising the off-spring, to animals where the customary roles are completely reversed.

Female sticklebacks put a lot of energy into producing their eggs, but it is the male who then guards against predators and against cannibalism by other sticklebacks. The parental investment of the male roughly balances the greater physiological contribution of the female, and both partners become near equals in the sexual process. To help the male in his task, he constructs a nest of weed and keeps the eggs aerated by fanning water over them. During courtship, male and female play their traditional roles. It is the male who does the wooing, displaying his bright red belly to the swollen females, and the female selects a mate who has a well-constructed nest in a protected site. Although the females make a choice about their mates, rejecting them if the nest is unsuitable, the males are no longer in endless supply, especially late in the season when many will already have their nests loaded with eggs. So the females fight between themselves, establishing a pecking order, the dominant females driving their subordinates from favourite nests and forcing them to mate with inferior males, occasionally preventing them from breeding altogether.

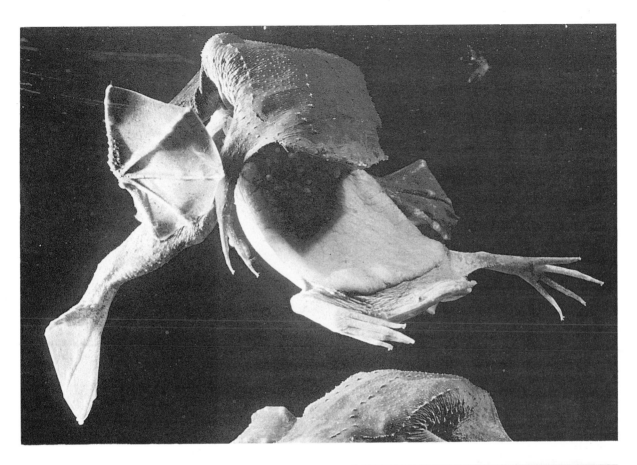

ABOVE AND RIGHT *Surinam toads mating (above). Here it is the female who carries the eggs on her back, while in the midwife toad (right) it is the male who carries strings of eggs wrapped around his hind legs. When eggs are fertilized externally, either parent can be left looking after them.*

OPPOSITE *Despite his contribution to looking after the young, the male stickleback still displays the bright colours typical of males, and initiates courtship.*

The male seahorse takes even greater responsibility for the young, carrying the eggs for a month in a special pouch on his belly. In these animals, the courtship roles are often reversed. Females carrying ripe eggs charge around nodding their heads provocatively at males and females alike, even at other species of seahorse, quite unusual behaviour when compared with the discrimination shown by the females of most other species. Courting animals intertwine their tails and swim about close to the sea bed, often for several hours, during which both partners become increasingly excited and presumably both make decisions about their choice of mate. Eventually the female lays her eggs into the male's belly pouch where he fertilizes them and protects them until the young are born.

When the parental roles are reversed and the male puts more effort into looking after the young than the female, he often tries very hard to make sure that all the offspring are really his. The female giant waterbug lays her eggs on the back of her mate, where he will carry them for over three weeks. As he swims around, the constant flow of water keeps the eggs aerated and prevents them from growing mouldy, but the load he carries must hamper his ability to forage for food and to escape quickly from predators. While he carries the eggs he cannot mate again, and when they are hatching, he stops feeding completely. When waterbugs mate, the female may still be carrying sperm from previous encounters and so to make certain that the young to which he will devote so much trouble are his own, the male copulates repeatedly. Every time she lays a few eggs on his back he interrupts her to top up her sperm storage sacs, burying the sperm of her previous mates beneath his own. One pair were seen to copulate more than a hundred times while the female transferred her 144 eggs to the mate's back, in an operation that lasted thirty-six hours.

Parental care by males and aggressive courtship by females is not

RIGHT *Male waterbug carrying eggs on his back.*

common, and it is rare for females to mate with several males. It is rarer still for females to defend their own territories or adopt the more extreme male strategies normally associated with animals like deer and elephant seals. Such a complete reversal of roles has so far been observed in only a very few species, most of them birds. This is surprising, since birds of course are internally fertilized, and it is by no means obvious why the male should end up with the work of looking after the young. Among monogamous birds it is quite common for males to share in the duties of incubation, freeing the female to feed and recover her strength after laying her eggs. If the female is so exhausted that she cannot cope with the demands of incubating, then males that forgo the advantages of chasing after other females and instead incubate the eggs themselves will be more successful. If the breeding season is long and there is no shortage of food, the female might recover in time to lay a second clutch and incubate it herself. Mountain plovers have this sort of breeding system. If the male is capable of fathering the second brood, the pair will remain faithful throughout the season; if not, the female will search for a new mate.

Where the female is able to mate again and leave the first clutch in the care of their father, the normal roles can be completely reversed. Males are in short supply and so the females fight between themselves

A male phalarope incubates his eggs.

The pugnacious female jacana threatens an intruder.

for opportunities to mate, and males choose whom they will mate with. The male Wilson's phalarope selects a suitable mate by swooping down over females and inviting them to chase him, inciting competition in rather the same way as the female mallard does when she encourages her mate to challenge other males. The female jacana, the only bird so far known to mate with several males yet enforce fidelity on all her partners, has evolved many of the characteristics usually associated with polygamous males. She is twice as heavy as her mates, and, unlike the females of most species, she is more brightly coloured than her partners. She holds a territory which she defends against other females in an attempt to keep them away from her mates, but she never incubates her own eggs, a task she leaves entirely to her males. She is, quite literally, a completely liberated bird; how does she get away with it?

This exceptional arrangement is born of exceptional circumstances. The jacana lives in central America and breeds on floating plants in the luxuriant marshes among the rainforest. Many clutches are lost through accidents to the unstable nests and their eggs and chicks are heavily preyed on by another marshland bird, the purple gallinule. Both sexes cooperate in protecting the nest, the female often standing guard when the male is away, but nonetheless many eggs are lost each year. The advantage of the jacana's female chauvinist mating system is that it allows the female bird to continue feeding throughout the breeding season and to lay several clutches of her small, cheaply produced eggs. Only by adopting such unusual mating behaviour have the jacanas ensured that at least some of their young will survive to breed the following year.

Parents and Teachers

Animals that protect their eggs can often make a considerable contribution to the survival of their young, but if they continue with their
care after the eggs have hatched or the young have been born, then the
stage is set for the evolution of a new skill. Such animals can also teach
their young the rudiments of survival.

Teaching must not be confused with learning. All sorts of animals
can learn. In fact it is an important part of individual survival for most
animals. Those creatures that never meet their parents must learn

everything for themselves, with no transmission of knowledge from one generation to the next. Parental care, evolved to reduce the death-rate of infants, makes it possible to pass this knowledge on. Even ducks and chickens whose young hatch with their eyes open, able to walk and swim almost immediately, will teach their offspring the rudiments of survival. A cat approaches and the mother hen gathers her brood beneath her, puffs herself up and challenges the intruder, protecting the young beneath her wings and at the same time teaching them that this furry, innocent-looking creature is dangerous. As the family feeds, the mother hen scratches around in places where she has

A mother hen teaches her chicks a good spot to search for food.

found food before and the young quickly learn that haystacks and compost heaps are good feeding spots.

Learning to distinguish friend, food and foe in the farmyard is fairly straightforward. In a tropical rainforest teeming with dangerous animals, many of them carefully disguised, the need to learn from parents is even greater. Young monkeys have an innate fear of snakes, even completely harmless ones, but their parents have been taught to distinguish the venomous snakes and in turn they pass this information on to their offspring. On seeing a snake, a young monkey panics immediately, jumping up and down with terror written all over its face. If the snake is no threat, the mother will sit quietly, perhaps with her foot on the youngster's tail to make sure that he does nothing stupid. If the snake is dangerous, she will pick up her baby and make a rapid exit. So it is from the way the mother responds that the youngster learns to distinguish harmless snakes from poisonous ones.

White storks usually migrate as family groups that join together in large flocks as they head south. Here too the experiences of the parents on previous flights help the young to find their way to the wintering grounds in central and southern Africa. White storks are soaring birds, riding on thermals to gain height and then gliding to the next rising column of air, a technique that makes their epic journey comparatively effortless. Over the sea there are no thermals, and so the birds from western Europe fly over Spain, cross the Mediterranean at Gibraltar, and head south along the west coast of Africa. Those from eastern Europe also keep to the land wherever possible, crossing the Bosphorus to fly down the east coast of the Mediterranean, across the Red Sea at its northern tip and then south over Ethiopia and the Sudan. Young birds from western Europe have an innate drive to fly south-westwards, which brings them to Spain. In Britain, white storks are extremely rare visitors, so a family artificially raised in Finland in 1971 caused some surprise when they appeared over central and southern England. One bird reached the Canary Islands, but there it died, exhausted by its flight over the water. These birds were following their instinctive south-westerly route, with catastrophic results.

Like many migrating birds, white storks are often blown wildly off course by sudden squalls, but birds that have made the journey before have somehow learned enough about their route to re-orientate themselves. Without help from their parents, unaided youngsters can make fatal mistakes, but when travelling in a family group or large flock they take the lead from their elders, avoiding disaster and learning the tricks themselves.

Animals can learn not only from their parents, but from any other individual with which they come into social contact, and so the transmission of information through teaching and learning differs fundamentally from the process of inheritance. Teaching, however, has a cost: it takes time, and a mother who passes on her knowledge to all and sundry improves the ability of her pupils to compete with her own offspring: a path to failure in the evolutionary struggle.

Parents clearly gain by helping their own young whenever they can.

The reflexes that bring a mother hen scuttling to her chicks when their squeaky, piping calls announce that danger is at hand are an innate response, genetically coded. Although the mother hen may be putting herself at risk by rushing to the aid of her brood, the instinct survives because more often than not she can protect her chicks without coming to any harm. Chicks that fail to inherit the genes that make this response possible will not make good mothers. In a sense, the genes are looking after themselves regardless of the fate of the individual that carries them. Suppose for instance that a hen in her native jungle home sees a snake and clucks a frightened alarm call. The bird's sister comes rushing to her aid, attacks the snake and is promptly swallowed whole. Swollen with its unexpectedly easy meal, the snake can stomach no more chicken and retires, leaving the bird that sounded the alarm unharmed. At first sight it seems that the process of natural selection should eliminate such suicidal behaviour, but in fact there is a good chance that the surviving bird carries the same set of genes that led to the demise of its sister. If the survivor goes on to raise a large family, then the genes that led to her sister's demise will actually increase in the population.

Of course, in the real world, things are not so simple. Biologists are only taking the very first steps in understanding how inherited characters actually affect behaviour. Although they presumably do not have genes that simply drive them into the jaws of predators, natural selection might well favour the survival of creatures that recognize snakes as dangerous and close relatives as creatures to be helped. Nor do hens need to sit down with an abacus to work out how much risk they should take for a second cousin once removed. Animals simply do as they feel and natural selection decides whether or not they made the right choice, favouring behaviour that increases the survival of those genes that made such behaviour possible.

However, many species do help their sisters and brothers. Two siblings are actually just as closely related as a parent and its young, but there are several reasons why help from siblings usually contributes less to raising the young than help from parents. Young animals can benefit enormously from help given by the parent, while littermates and nest-mates are equally helpless and often unable to improve each other's chances of survival. Once the brood or litter is mature, the young animals are more likely to spread their genes successfully by themselves reproducing than by helping their sisters to do so. However, animals can contribute more to the survival of their sisters if they help to raise subsequent broods. The problem here is that it is often difficult for potential helpers to be certain that the next brood consists of full sisters and not half sisters.

There are situations when an animal will definitely do better by staying to help its parents raise future generations than by breeding itself. Among birds, helpers at the nest are quite common. For example Florida scrub jays, as their name suggests, live in oak scrub where ownership of breeding territories is fiercely contested. Many families stay together for several years, the young birds supporting their

OPPOSITE *A group of red-throated bee-eaters (Merops nubicus) that have been helping to raise a single clutch of eggs.*

parents. Seven or eight birds may help to raise a single brood, the helpers easing their parents' workload by bringing food. Also, they contribute significantly to the chances of successfully rearing the brood by helping to defend the nest against snakes, and giving alarm calls to warn the chicks whenever danger threatens.

Mammalian helpers are much rarer, but they are not unknown. Among several species of mongoose, young animals help their parents or relatives by baby-sitting while the pack is hunting, or by sounding alarm calls when danger threatens. Female dwarf mongooses may even lactate and begin feeding their younger sisters and brothers, although they will not themselves breed successfully until the top-ranking female in the pack dies.

By helping to raise their brothers and sisters, scrub jays and mongooses contribute to the survival of their own genes and also learn the rudiments of raising young, knowledge that will be useful when their turn comes to breed.

Social Insects

Alone among every species of living thing the bees have children which are common to all. All inhabit the same dwelling, and work together . . . procreation and virginity are in common and so is birth, for they suddenly produce the greatest swarm of progeny, picking up grubs with the mouth from leaves and grasses. They arrange their own king, but although they are placed under a king, they are perfectly free.

We have come a long way in our understanding of bees since the 12th-century monk wrote the Latin bestiary from which this extract is taken. The passage reflects many of the prejudices of its time. Not until late in the 17th century was the king recognized as queen and mother of the colony, spoiling the allegory of the bee as a chaste and industrious creature willing to die selflessly for its lord and master. Yet out of the errors and misconceptions, one single line still rings true. Bees have children that are common to all. The queen is the genetic mother of the colony, but the workers perform all the parental duties, feeding the young and protecting them from predators. In cold weather they sit shivering to generate heat and keep the nest warm. As the colony heats up on a summer's day, they beat their wings and fan fresh air across their brood. Just why do the workers devote so much of their time and energy to raising someone else's young, and why has this strange social behaviour evolved repeatedly in the bees, wasps and ants, but only once in all the other insect groups?

Surprisingly, the answer to both questions may depend on the peculiar genetics of sex in the bees, wasps and ants (collectively called the Hymenoptera). Female hymenopterans, like most insects, are diploid organisms that inherit a set of chromosomes from both parents. But the males are unusual and develop from unfertilized, haploid eggs. This completely confuses our conventional understanding of family relations. For example as the diagram shows, male bees are usually completely unrelated to the male who fertilized their mother, while the workers are more closely related to each other than to their mother or father. Importantly, since the queens produced by a colony are full sisters of the workers in that colony, those workers are more closely related to their sister-queens than they would be to their own offspring. Consequently their genes will best be represented in the next generation if they forgo the opportunity to lay eggs themselves and work together to raise their sisters, for among their sisters will be the next generation of queen bees.

This explanation for the evolution of social behaviour is beautifully elegant, and, were it not for the termites, the story would end here. We have already seen that even in animals whose sex is determined by more orthodox methods, siblings are just as closely related to each other as to their own offspring. Even without the peculiar genetics of the hymenoptera, animals might in theory spread their genes more rapidly by remaining chaste or sterile and devoting themselves to the care of their sisters or brothers.

OPPOSITE Worker bumble-bee warming a pupa.

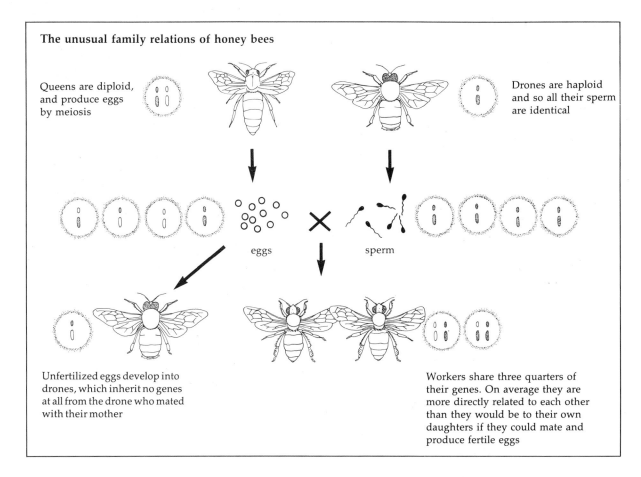

The unusual family relations of honey bees

Queens are diploid, and produce eggs by meiosis

Drones are haploid and so all their sperm are identical

eggs × sperm

Unfertilized eggs develop into drones, which inherit no genes at all from the drone who mated with their mother

Workers share three quarters of their genes. On average they are more directly related to each other than they would be to their own daughters if they could mate and produce fertile eggs

Inside a wasps' nest.

Termites belong to a completely different group of insects, more closely related to the cockroaches than to the wasps and bees; both males and females are normal diploid animals and their sex is determined in the same way as in many other insects, females having two X chromosomes and males only one (see under 'Males and Females'). Yet their social structure is similar to that of the social hymenoptera. There are castes of worker termites, which cooperate to build the nest, feed and protect the young and to control the nest's internal environment. All the eggs are laid by a single, massively swollen queen who is completely incapable of looking after herself and is tended entirely by the workers.

Although the structure of termite society is similar to that of other social insects, there are some interesting differences. Workers and drones in a bees' nest are only distantly related to each other, and the drones, who have become a metaphor for laziness, do nothing to help their sisters. In a termite nest, workers are both male and female and both help with the task of raising the brood. This supports the theory that these animals are transmitting their genes by helping their relatives, since, in termites, males and females are both just as closely related to the future queens, and both have as much to gain by their success. A similar pattern is found in the only mammals that seem to have a completely sterile worker caste, the naked mole-rats from East Africa. These animals spend their entire lives in underground burrows, feeding on bulbs and tubers and unlike most subterranean mammals they live in large colonies, probably extended families. Uniquely, only one female breeds and she is helped by animals that are themselves incapable of breeding. If the breeding female is removed, she is replaced not from the 'worker caste' but from a small group of non-workers who are larger than the workers but do little to help look after the colony.

While the peculiar genetics of the hymenopterans have made it possible for their complex social system to evolve separately several times within this group, it is clear that this unusual genetic system is not an essential pre-requisite for the evolution of social behaviour.

Sex and Society

A wise member of the public once pinned a notice to a small and miserable cage in which sat a single chimpanzee. The notice read 'One chimpanzee is not a chimpanzee'. Only by watching a troop of chimps in a large enclosure can the profound truth of this simple statement really be appreciated. Chimps, like baboons and most other social animals, are in a state of constant activity, feeding and moving about their range, but above all interacting with each other by grooming, playing, squabbling and occasionally mating. Their complicated behaviour is as much a part of being a chimpanzee as the shape of their bodies or the colour of their fur.

Many animals live together in groups for at least a part of their lives;

Barbary macaques grooming.

tits, finches and many other birds often flock together outside the breeding season, gaining better protection from predators through their combined watchfulness. In the flocks of starlings that twist and turn through the autumn sky, the birds seem to move as one, yet in spring the flock disintegrates and the birds breed independently. For animals to live together permanently, they must somehow overcome the disruptive effects of sexual competition. Among the simplest animals like the algae or the corals, there is no cause for competition between the individuals that make up the colony since the colony is a clone, produced by asexual reproduction and each member contains an identical set of chromosomes. Their genes will be most successfully reproduced if the colony works together efficiently, and so some cells become specialized and give up their reproductive role altogether. The workers in colonies of bees or wasps cooperate for the same reasons, securing the future of their genes by pardoxically giving up the opportunity to reproduce themselves and concentrating instead on maintaining the whole colony. The 'societies' of bees, wasps and corals are based on an impersonal interdependence, devoid of the

205

There are many possible reasons for living together in groups or breeding cooperatively. A group of ostriches lay their eggs in a single nest which is then incubated by the dominant female with help from her mate. The brooding female can recognize her own eggs, and if there are too many in the nest for her to brood, she pushes the eggs of other females out. If the nest is found by a predator, the eggs around the edge are the first it encounters. A single ostrich egg is a good meal for most animals, so the eggs of the dominant female are unlikely to be attacked.

African village weaverbirds nest in colonies because the savannah provides plenty of food but few trees to nest in. In such dense aggregations, and with easy access to food, polygamy is the favoured strategy. In the forest, the weaverbird's insect-eating relatives are solitary and monogamous.

Lackey moth caterpillars will remain together until they pupate. Their bright colours warn of an unpleasant surprise for any animal foolish enough to try and eat them. Naive birds may take a single caterpillar, but once tasted, these are never forgotten. The unfortunate caterpillar that gets eaten gives up its life for its relatives who share the same genes for bright colours.

intimacy that is implied when we refer to a troop of baboons as a society. What distinguishes the baboon troop is that their society is bonded not just by the mutual cooperation of close relatives, but by a more complicated network of personal alliances between both related and unrelated animals. Bees and wasps recognize only the caste of other insects in their colony, but in a baboon troop animals recognize each other as individuals.

In such cases there is a social hierarchy and, for instance, a female baboon will spend more time grooming other females of similar status

Ruddy mongooses mating. Many mongooses live in groups, which include members of the same family and immigrants from other groups. In many species the dominant male and female are parents of all the offspring, and although the male may mate with several females, the dominant female will kill all the pups of her subordinates. However, the structure of the mongooses' social system is flexible. In other species several high-ranking animals will breed, while ruddy mongooses are solitary, and the young are raised by their parents without any help at all.

than she will spend on animals from different social strata. Often animals that occupy similar ranks in the society are closely related, but not always. Being groomed is undoubtedly of immediate, practical advantage because a partner can remove parasites from inaccessible areas of the coat and clean dirt and debris from wounds. There is also a cost to the animal that does the work since of course grooming takes time that could otherwise be spent searching for food or courting. By grooming unrelated animals, however, baboons help forge alliances that they will use when competing with other members of the troop.

The importance of alliances has been clearly demonstrated by a study of olive baboons in east Africa. Adult male olive baboons often enlist the support of other males during disputes. For instance, if a male is consorting with an estrous female, he will occasionally be attacked and driven away by a pair of males, one of which then mates with the female. The successful male is inevitably the male who began the attack, but the male whose aid he enlisted will in turn be able to call for help from his ally when he finds himself in a similar situation. Baboons like many other social animals have grasped the concept of the fair deal and will spend time helping others, not because they are genetically related, but because the alliance will be of practical use in the future.

In a troop of baboons, as in most social animals, the ties that bind the group are difficult to unravel and the methods being used to study social behaviour are often still crude and clumsy. It is gradually becoming clear that a cohesive mammalian society is bound together in several different ways. The parents (particularly the mother, who can be certain of her genetic relationship with the young) protect, groom, teach and support their offspring. This is not uncommon among animals generally, but social mammals also forge alliances with unrelated individuals that improve their own chances of survival. The possible trade in benefits may be even more complex. For example, female vervet monkeys will allow unrelated females to look after their young, gaining a brief respite from the ties of motherhood in return for allowing a sometimes young and inexperienced female to 'practise' being a mother on someone else's baby. It will take many more uncomfortable years of painstaking observation in the field before biologists can explain why this trade-off is worthwhile for vervet monkeys, but unacceptable to mother macaques or chimpanzees whose young are trusted only to elder daughters.

Any statement about sex and sexuality
in our complex society is bound to be
controversial.

chapter ten

Human Sex

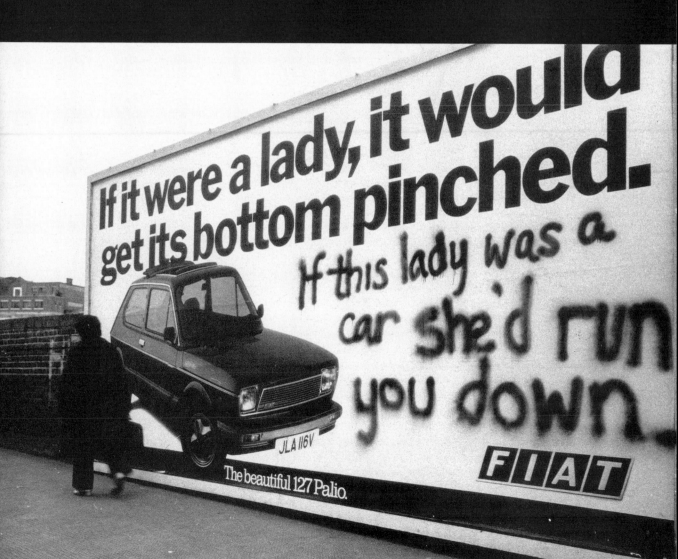

Sex and Human Nature

'Both mice and people mate in order to have babies' could be a line taken from any number of elementary sex books for children. Certainly one thing leads to another, but if this were strictly true the world would surely be a duller place. To try and explain our behaviour in terms of its ultimate biological function is obviously a ridiculous over-simplification, yet to compare human and animal biology in this way is attractive for several reasons. Those of us fortunate enough to be living in the industrialized countries are largely isolated from the natural world. In these countries, only a small proportion of the population is involved directly in growing food, even fewer in hunting. We are protected by our technology from heat and cold, even from the painful realities of birth and death. Society has grown overwhelming in its complexity and has alienated itself from nature. Part of the fascination of behavioural biology is that it promises to explain our human behaviour in terms of biological realities, to remove the division between human and animal. It promises to peel away the artifice and show us our true selves.

This promise alone is irresistible, but so too is the challenge that human behavioural biology poses to students of animal behaviour. By studying human behaviour, biologists hope to test their theories about animals, as well as to gain insight into why we behave as we do. Such scientific speculations may seem harmless enough, especially since biologists are generally sympathetic and well-meaning people, but they have sparked off some of the most bitter rows in modern biology and the heated arguments now echo through the fields of sociology, education and politics. Why then is the study of the biological basis of human behaviour, and in particular human sexual behaviour, so contentious?

One reason is that some of the conclusions to which simplistic biological theories lead are quite unpleasant. Imagine for a moment a poor human male, destitute and landless, living in a society which provides no help for families who cannot afford to feed their children. Were he to marry and start a family, his children would starve. In sharing their meagre food with a child, the parents might also starve themselves. He is intelligent and well aware that the resources in his society are already allocated and fiercely defended. He has nothing and there is no way in which he can improve his position. If, like the animals we have discussed throughout this book, he were biologically programmed to raise as many young as possible, what should he do? One strategy which might ensure biological success would be to seduce or rape rich women.

This scenario of course is over-simplified and bears little relation to present realities, but this style of reasoning has recently become unpleasantly popular. The sort of conclusion to which it can lead shows why the debate about the biological basis of human social behaviour has become so bitter. Working from the assumption that humans as animals have an innate drive to expand their family tree leads to some very unpleasant predictions about how we might expect people to behave.

There are of course many unpleasant facts of life, not least among them the fact of our own mortality. Our own death is inevitable and we must accept it, yet we fight it with medicines, with surgery, with programmes for community health, with laws about hygiene, even with dreams of immortality. The inevitability, the naturalness of death does not prevent us from taking every step to see that it is delayed as long as possible. However, unlike death, the rape of women is not inevitable. It is prevented by our culture, by our laws and by our human ability to sympathize with our fellow mortals. For us humans, our culture can override our nature.

Even if our genes do not exclusively determine our behaviour, looking at humans and animals in this way still leaves us with a pessimistic view of human nature, a view which can be used to justify harsh, repressive legal measures, even compulsory sterilization and genocide. Once again, if the nature of the human animal is something so fundamentally offensive, then there is nothing for it but to swallow hard and decide what social and legal measures are necessary to make human beings fit into society. But it is by no means certain that humans possess such instinctive drives, and anyway to draw such inferences is to misunderstand the process of science and to give it a reverence that it does not deserve. The body of scientific knowledge is continually changing as old theories are disproved and amended and new theories are developed. Even Darwin's 125-year-old theory of evolution is constantly being adjusted to include new information and modified in response to new questions. Such shifting sands are dangerous foundations for a theory of human behaviour. To act on the basis of such a theory could have profound political and social consequences. Ultimately, comparative social biology can prove nothing about human nature, it can only provide theories consistent with the observed facts. It is not impossible that the world really was created by a supreme being; that chimpanzees love one another; or that dolphins are the most intelligent life-form on the planet but are wisely keeping the information to themselves. Such beliefs cannot be disproved, they are simply not testable.

These criticisms should make us cautious. Our nature may limit the ways in which we can behave, but it cannot lead us inevitably to a course of action. In addition, any theory that we develop will be the subject of later changes, revisions and additions. Man is an animal and has (presumably) evolved from ape-like ancestors which behaved as animals, pursuing their basic biological goal of leaving behind them as many viable offspring as possible. Bearing in mind the previous words of caution, what if anything can we say about the nature of human sexuality?

Humans have almost the lowest reproductive rate in the animal kingdom, giving birth to single children at intervals of several years. Children are dependent on their mother's milk for two years or so, and rely on their parents for food and protection for considerably longer.

Like the young of other slowly reproducing animals, children need continual care if they are to grow to maturity and establish themselves in society as adults and, most importantly, as parents.

Human children are unusually dependent on their parents, but this is not the only way in which our reproductive biology differs from that of other animals. The nature of the human reproductive cycle itself is unusual. Most animals, as we have seen, organize their sexual activity so that mating occurs when the female is receptive, and matings are usually fertile. Through pheromones and visual displays, females go to considerable lengths to advertise their sexual state to males, announcing the moment at which mating will be most productive. For example a cow will attract bulls for only about half a day in every three weeks, and only during this brief period will she tolerate being mated. While she is in heat, her behaviour changes; she is restless, she walks about more and she attempts to mount other cows. In cats, mating induces the female to release the egg into the oviduct, but she still demonstrates her readiness to mate by a period of heat, during which she releases pheromones and solicits mating by her characteristic posturing. Female primates, like humans, have a rhythmic sexual cycle which involves menstruation, yet unlike humans the other primates all signal their sexual status. Female chimps and baboons display their swollen rumps when in heat. Macaque monkeys produce pheromones which arouse sexual interest in the males. The orangutan communicates its readiness to mate through its behaviour. Although copulation occurs throughout the sexual cycle in all these animals, sexual activity is concentrated around the period in which conception is most likely.

Women, uniquely, appear not to advertise when they ovulate, even

A female chacma baboon in estrus displays her swollen genital area. Unlike humans, most animals make it quite clear when they are sexually receptive.

though this seems remarkably counterproductive if the main purpose of sex is to produce young.

Sociobiologists have proposed many theories to explain why our ancestors lost these signals. For instance, it has been suggested that females concealed their estrus in order to bribe males into providing food in return for sexual favours, enabling them to nurse their infants for longer periods. An alternative idea is that conspicuous advertising was the last thing that the protohuman female wanted, since aggressive competition between males can be dangerous for the female. Yet although women do not display estrus in the same way as chimps, their cycle is not completely cryptic. Some women are consciously aware of the day on which they ovulate and feel increased sexual arousal at this time. Some rather bizarre physiological changes take place. Experiments have shown that women become more sensitive to the smell of musk during ovulation than they are throughout the rest of their cycle and may be more alert generally. Importantly, such changes can be detected by others. Women living in close contact with each other tend to synchronize their menstrual cycles. Eventually, over a period of months, the cycles of close friends and room-mates move into step, even though they may not be consciously aware of each other's menstrual rhythm. Remarkably, smell seems to be the cue that makes this possible.

Whatever the mechanism that makes women aware of each other's cycles, it is very unlikely that men cannot read the same messages. Our male ape-ancestors that learnt to do this would have been at an advantage in the evolutionary struggle, for they could have prepared themselves for the right moment. If, however, they could tell when their band was fertile but found no advantage in being promiscuous, then what was the advantage of making the estrus signals so subtle?

An alternative explanation is that the inconspicuous sexual cycle in women is part of the process which helps to maintain the bond between a child's parents, and this long-term bond is obviously useful if the arduous task of raising the child is to be completed successfully. Although women are often more easily aroused around the moment of ovulation, sex can be pleasurable throughout the cycle. Once the protohuman female ceased to provide conspicuous signals to which males reponded by mating, sex could be released from its primary function of procreation to perform a secondary function of helping to maintain the bond between the partners. This idea has been criticized on the grounds that other monogamous animals, like the gibbon and the fox, are no more active sexually than closely related polygamous species. These animals, however, live as independent family groups, and monogamy is maintained quite effectively by the aggression of neighbouring territory holders towards intruders.

Why should a man stay exclusively with one woman? The traditional view is certainly that our ancestors did no such thing, but that like male chimps, protohuman males were promiscuous and vied with each other for access to females, while females accepted any male capable of fighting his way through the competition. Lucretius, the

Roman philosopher, may have been responsible for starting this idea nearly two thousand years ago, when he wrote that 'lacking the institution of marriage, early man followed a career of sexual promiscuity'. The view was accepted by Darwin, Freud and is still popular with many biologists, but its origins lie in the prejudice that Nature could not have devised anything more sophisticated. We can now see that this is not necessarily true. Animals may be strictly monogamous, polygamous, promiscuous, sexless, or some combination of these, depending on their lifestyle. If the first upright apes were not necessarily promiscuous, then what might their mating system have been?

Imagine a protohuman band moving about the African savannah where our ancestors made their home, acting as a single social unit. In this group, it is probable that most of the females would menstruate in synchrony with each other, as women in similar situations tend to today. This synchronous cycle might once have been reinforced by the moon. The average length of the human menstrual cycle is exactly 29.5 days, the length of a lunar month. While it is possible that this is coincidence or even a relic of our tidal past, it seems unlikely that such a precise match could be maintained over such a long period of time if it served no function. The length of the cycle in apes is similar to ours (31 days in gorillas, 30 in chimps and 30.5 days in orang-utans), but it varies widely in other primates, from 9 days in the squirrel monkey to 40 in the ring-tailed lemur. A further coincidence is that the period of gestation in humans is exactly nine lunar months and it has been suggested that the lunar month is a biologically fundamental time-period for humans. There is also evidence of a slight but significant increase in conceptions (and presumably ovulations) at the time of the full moon, all of which taken together might suggest that our ancestors synchronized their sexual cycle with the phases of the moon and ovulated when it was full.

Lunar synchronization might appear symbolic, magical or even romantic, conjuring up attractive fantasies of passion beneath a Neanderthal moon. The real reason is probably more prosaic. If for some reason it was important that women menstruated in synchrony, what other external cue could they synchronize with? A yearly estrus cycle is common enough, but leaves a very long cooling-off period, perhaps unnecessary in an animal with such elaborately developed systems of parental care. A daily cycle is too short for any mammal to stand the pace. Like Goldilocks' porridge, the lunar cycle is neither too long nor too short but just right.

There is evidence from studies of early human cultures that the synchronization of the menstrual cycle continued well beyond the time of our prehuman ancestors and was widespread in many societies until relatively recently, often reinforced by complex rituals. Above a Yurok Indian village in California is a 'sacred moon pond' where menstruating women once went to bathe. According to local legends, all the women of the household menstruated together, and if a woman lost her synchrony with the other members of her group, she would go and sit in the moonlight and ask the moon to balance her. In

Australia, rock paintings show groups of women dancing together and menstruating, and the Aboriginal rainbow serpent myth tells of two sisters who in order to keep the rainbow serpent at bay danced together until both began to menstruate. Taken together with evidence from many other groups it is clear that synchronous menstruation was once very important in primitive cultures.

Drawings of Aboriginal rock paintings, from the Pilbara region of Australia, show women dancing and menstruating (1,4). In two of the pictures (2,5) women are symbolically joined by their menstrual blood, while in 3 the blood turns into a serpent, a symbol perhaps of the cyclic nature of the menses. The Aborigines tell a story about the Wawilak sisters who at the beginning of time gave names to a previously unnamed world, and who battled with the Rainbow Serpent. The serpent is a mythological beast that represents the womens' menstrual blood, and the tie that binds women together.

'So the younger sister began to dance, to hinder the Snake's progress. The rainbow serpent stopped in her course, and watched the dancing. But the girl grew tired and called out: 'Come on, sister, your turn now. I want to rest.' The older sister came from the hut, leaving her child behind in its soft cradle of paperbark, and began to dance. But her blood, still intermittently flowing, attracted the snake further, and she moved towards them.

'Come on sister,' cried the elder, 'It's no good for me; my blood is coming out and the snake is smelling it and coming closer. It is better for you to go on dancing.'

So the younger sister continued, and again the Rainbow Serpent stopped and watched . . . in this way the sisters took it in turns to dance; when the younger sister danced, the snake stopped; but when the older one continued she came forward again. So the younger girl danced longer than the other, and as she swayed from side to side the intensive activity caused her menstruation to begin; then the python, smelling more blood, came forward without hesitation.'

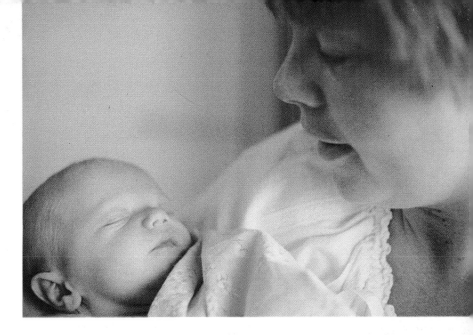

OPPOSITE A lioness and her cub. In a pride, all the lionesses come into heat at the same time.

RIGHT Human infants form a unique bond with their parents. As in all mammals, the newborn baby is dependent on its mother's milk; but unlike most animals, the father is also able to contribute to the care and protection of the young. The cooperation of both parents helps the child to assimilate the wealth of knowledge necessary if it is to integrate itself into the society.

If through using odour cues reinforced by the lunar cycle, proto-human females synchronized their sexual cycle with other members of their group, males would gain very little by trying to mate with more than one female. A similar system has evolved in lions, where often two or three males control a single pride of up to a dozen females. Females come into heat in synchrony and are surprisingly infertile, and a male mates every twenty-five minutes or so throughout the period when the lioness is receptive. Consequently the males have little to gain by competing with each other for access to females.

Lions, of course, are not monogamous; the males that control a pride can exclude bachelor males and keep an unequal share of the females to themselves. If the sex ratio of the protohuman band was nearer to unity, then a man who left his mate during the short period of syn-chronous ovulation to search for other females would be risking cuckoldry. Also he might be attacked by other, more faithful males, and all with little prospect of actually fathering a child. While much of the evidence is circumstantial, it is easy to see that unlike the lions our ape-man ancestors could indeed have been monogamous.

Consistent with this theory, monogamy is the commonest type of bond in present human society. Only a minority of cultures actually forbid polygamy, but in most it remains the exception rather than the rule. But to compare monogamy in present societies with monogamy in our hypothetical protohuman ancestral band is like trying to compare ritual courtship in birds with the subtleties of after-dinner conversation. Even among peoples that survive by hunting and gathering, and who use few tools, peoples in which the structure of society might be closest to that of our ancestral band, monogamy means far more than simply the natural tendency to copulate with only one chosen mate. It means a formal alliance, marriage, recognized and respected by the rest of society, often intimately connected with that society's religious beliefs. This alliance has important consequences. It gives the offspring legitimate rights, and forms an essential part of

the legal structure which determines how goods and land are transferred from generation to generation. It determines to which social group a child belongs, on whom he or she can call for help and to whom he or she owes allegiance. In all societies, marriage involves some degree of mutual obligation; it involves a commitment to each other and the offspring above and beyond the selfish drives which nature selects, and the bond it creates is expected to last beyond the birth and feeding of the young and for some time afterwards.

Formal marriage is universal in human society, but it is not always a monogamous affair. Some biologists have argued that the differences in stature between men and women, and the other physical differences between the sexes, imply that humans are adapted to a low level of polygamy. Where a single man can control enough resources to support several women, and where this type of alliance helps the women to raise more children, then polygamy will be adopted. This is analogous with the situation in many polygamous animals. Where a male can control many females and mate with them, then he will. The determinants of polygamy in human societies, however, are far, far more complex than the process of natural selection which operates in other animals. The structure of the human family group is determined not merely by how many wives the father can support. It is determined by religion, traditon and the legal structure of the society, that is by its culture. The structure of the family group is, above all else, flexible. In Britain and North America, the extended family, in which aunts, uncles and cousins cooperated in the raising of children, has recently been substantially replaced by the nuclear family, where parents raise their children almost in isolation. In much of Africa and the Middle East, polygamous marriages are becoming rarer as new

China, with a present population of approximately 7,000,000,000 is one of keenly aware of the social disruption that results when resources cannot support the population. Restricting family size is a serious personal sacrifice for peasant peoples whose security in old age often depends on a thriving family. But however reluctantly, most Chinese bow to the pressures of their society and now raise only a single child in each family. Making such a sacrifice for the good of the group requires a level of social organization unknown in other animals.

ideas about the rights of women infiltrate the culture. In many cultures, bisexuality has long been approved; only recently has it been acknowledged as an acceptable sexual practice in the west. Most remarkably, humans practice contraception, limiting the size of their family not just to the number of children they know that they can support, but to a number that is determined by the whole society as being socially acceptable. Humanity can and does behave as a group, not only as a collection of selfish individuals. Unlike animals, we have the power to think not only of ourselves, our genes and our family line, but to act cohesively as a society to achieve what is best for the group as a whole. It is the irony of our individual consciousness that it allows us to realize that only through sacrificing any selfish drive to extend our family tree can we guarantee a future for that family.

This may be labouring the point, but the point is of paramount importance. Humans do not transmit only genes. They also transmit their culture, and not only to their children but to anyone with whom they communicate. Humans can even die for a cause. Biologically this is an act of suicide, but human history is the story of martyrs whose ideas have influenced their societies long after their death. By contrast, to return to an earlier example, the rapist cannot possibly be excused because he is fulfilling some imagined innate drive to ensure that his genes survive. It is doubtful whether such a biological urge exists in humans, since rape is unknown in many cultures, but common in others. And in losing his sense of sympathy with his victim, the rapist has become, in a very real sense, less than human. It is incidental that he has also broken the social code to which he must adhere if his offspring are to compete effectively with their peers.

Human sexual behaviour is characterized by its flexibility. Whatever the mating behaviour of our ancestors, our species has now altered so much that our behaviour cannot be explained simply as a means towards greater reproductive ends. It may be possible, if we choose, to remove the last vestiges of our biological past, and move into a 'Brave New World' where children are raised in incubators and men and women really do become merely the genetic parents of their offspring. Hormone implants could remove all but the most fundamental anatomical differences between men and women. This version of the future may be undesirable for all sorts of reasons, but it is possible. Alternatively we could continue our present social experimentation, our monogamous, polygamous, homo- and hetero-sexual cultures and subcultures. The choice is ours.

Illustration sources

Mike Amphlett, Oxford: 100
Ardea, London: 8-9 (Arthus-Bertrand): 12-13 (John Clegg); 28 (François Gohier); 39 (J.L. Mason); 57 (J.B. and S. Bottomley); 59 (J.L. Mason); 64 (François Gohier); 67 (Ian Beames); 72-3 (Ron and Valerie Taylor); 83 (Ian Beames); 95; 104 (Bob Gibbons); 106 (Tom Willock); 121 (Adrian Warren); 128 (*top*) (Alan Weaving); 147 (Alan Beames); 158-9 (Hans and Judy Beste, Australia); 162 (P. Morris); 163 (*top*) (Eric Lindgren); 166-7 (Åke Lindau); 167 (Åke Lindau); 178-9 (Liz and Tony Bomford); 178 (*below*) (Liz and Tony Bomford); 185 (*top*) (François Gohier); 205 (Jean-Paul Ferrero); 214 (Clem Haagner)
Sue Baker: 19; 20; 21; 33 (*above*); 41; 47; 70 (*above*); 111; 113; 200; 217
Rodney Borland: 93 (*below*)
Julia Brooke-White: 74
Bruce Coleman Limited: 30-1 (*top*) (Manfred Kage); 68 (Jane Burton); 91 (*right*) (Eric Crichton); 128 (*bottom*) (A.J. Deane); 130-1 (Jane Burton); 132 (*left*) (Jane Burton); 185 (*below*) (Dieter and Mary Plage); 190 (Jane Burton)
Andrew Crump: 219
Martin Dohrn: 30-1 (*below*); 87; 105; 108-9; 138-9 (*below*)
Frank Lane Picture Agency Limited: *Frontispiece*; 83

(Len Rue, Jr); 129 (Len Rue, Jr); 132 (*right*) (Mark Newman); 133 (Philip Perry); 136 (Winfried Wisniewski); 157 (G.W. Elison); 164-5 (Winfried Wisniewski)
© Dr C. Fry: 155, 198
Gower Medical Publishing Limited: 15; 16
© Green Films Limited: 55 (Chris Catton); 58 (Tony Allen); 59 (*below*) (Chris Catton); 63 (Tony Allen); 65 (Chris Catton); 70 (*below*) (Chris Catton); 77 (Tony Allen); 85 (*top*) (Chris Catton); 112 (*top*) (Chris Catton); 122 (*below*) (Tony Allen); 124 (2) (Chris Catton); 142 (Chris Catton); 147 (Tony Allen); 149 (Tony Allen); 153 (Chris Catton); 154 (Chris Catton); 170-1 (Tony Allen); 182 (Tony Allen); 184 (Tony Allen); 192 (Tony Allen); 194-5 (Tony Allen); 201 (Tony Allen); 207 (*below*) (Tony Allen)
Heather Angel: 36-7; 42-3; 69; 75; 79; 112 (*below*), 116-7; 126; 150-1; 176; 189 (*top*); 189 (*below*); 202-3
John Topham Picture Library: 220
Bertil Kullenberg, Sweden: 93 (*top*)
Dr J. Mackinnon: 144
Natural History Photographic Agency: 40 (Stephen Dalton); 44 (N.A. Callow); 52-3 (Stephen Dalton); 56 (Ivan Polunin); 163 (*below right*) (Ivan Polunin); 193 (Haroldo Palo, Jr)
Nature Photographers Limited: 80-1; 84; 85 (*below*)

(Charles Palmer); 96-7 (Owen Newman); 103 (D. Swindells); 156 (Thomas Ennis); 160; 207 (*top*) (Derek Scott) © Owen Newman: 134; 139 (*right*)
Oxford Scientific Films: *Half-Title* (Stephen Dalton); 17; 25 (Peter Parks); 48-9; 92 (Tim Shepherd); 119 (G.I. Bernard); 146 (G.I. Bernard)
William B. Preston, Manitoba, Canada: 89
Jill Posener, c/o The Women's Press, 124 Shoreditch High Street, London E1: 211 'London 1979'
Tracy Scaysbrooke: 169
Science Photo Library: 122 (*top*) (Martin Dohrn)
Seaphot Limited: Planet Earth Pictures: 29 (Mike Coltman); 33 (*below*); 36 (Peter David); 76 (Peter Scoones); 86 (Walter Deas); 114 (K. Ammann); 138-9 (*top*) (Nigel Downer); 177 (Chris Howes); 180 (Chris Howes); 186-7 (Julian Hector); 206 (Sean Avery); 218 (Jonathan Scott)
R.L. Smith: 191
Soames/Summerhays/Biofotos: 38
Sólarfilma, Reykjavik, Iceland: 23
Survival Anglia: 208 (Dieter and Mary Plage)
Susan Griggs Agency Limited: 172-3 (Jonathan Blair)
Lord Christopher Thynne: 11
Dr Merlin D. Tuttle: 60-1
Victoria and Albert Museum, London: 125

Index